T0150341

What Lies Ahead

for America's Children
and Their Schools

*The Hoover Institution gratefully acknowledges the following individuals
and foundations for their significant support of the*

INITIATIVE ON AMERICAN PUBLIC EDUCATION AND THE HOOVER INSTITUTION'S KORET TASK FORCE ON K–12 EDUCATION

KORET FOUNDATION

TAD AND DIANNE TAUBE

TAUBE FAMILY FOUNDATION

Lynde and Harry Bradley Foundation
John M. Olin Foundation
William E. Simon Foundation
The Bernard Lee Schwartz Foundation, Inc.
Jack R. and Mary Lois Wheatley

James E. Bass
Stephen Bechtel Fund
Dean A. Cortopassi
Earhart Foundation
Doris and Donald Fisher
The JM Foundation
Franklin and Catherine Johnson
The Honorable and Mrs. Howard H. Leach
Edmund and Jeannik Littlefield
The Packard Humanities Institute
Ronald B. Rankin
The Smart Family Foundation Inc.
Boyd and Jill Smith
Thomas and Barbara Stephenson
The Honorable Robert D. Stuart Jr.
Chris T. Sullivan
Walton Family Foundation, Inc.
James S. Whitcomb
Zachariah P. Zachariah, M.D.

What Lies Ahead
for America's Children
and Their Schools

**Edited by Chester E. Finn Jr.
and Richard Sousa**

with an Introduction by Chester E. Finn Jr.

HOOVER INSTITUTION PRESS
STANFORD UNIVERSITY   STANFORD, CALIFORNIA

The Hoover Institution on War, Revolution and Peace, founded at Stanford University in 1919 by Herbert Hoover, who went on to become the thirty-first president of the United States, is an interdisciplinary research center for advanced study on domestic and international affairs. The views expressed in its publications are entirely those of the authors and do not necessarily reflect the views of the staff, officers, or Board of Overseers of the Hoover Institution.

www.hoover.org

An imprint of the Hoover Institution Press

Hoover Institution Press Publication No. 644

First printing 2014
21 20 19 18 17 16 15 14   9 8 7 6 5 4 3 2 1

Manufactured in the United States of America

The paper used in this publication meets the minimum
Requirements of the American National Standard for Information
Sciences—Permanence of Paper for Printed Library Materials,
ANSI/NISO Z39.48-1992. ∞

Cataloging-in-Publication Data is available from the Library
of Congress.
ISBN-13: 978-0-8179-1705-0 (pbk. : alk. paper)
ISBN-13: 978-0-8179-1706-7 (e-book)
ISBN-13: 978-0-8179-1707-4 (mobi)
ISBN-13: 978-0-8179-1708-1 (PDF)

Contents

Foreword

"He who fails to plan is planning to fail"
—Winston Churchill

One of the most important elements in economic productivity growth—if not *the most important* element—is human capital development. At the foundation of human capital development is a solid footing in K–12 education. Sadly, that solid footing in the United States is, at best, crumbling and, at worst, barely standing.

In an increasingly complex global economy, providing the highest-quality education to tomorrow's leaders is crucial if the United States is to maintain its competitive edge and its position as the world's leading economic power. The public recognizes this. Although lists of citizens' concerns are still topped by national security and combating terrorism, government gridlock and potential financial default, and stubbornly high unemployment and a persistently underperforming economy, American parents and the general public still worry about how well (or poorly) we educate our children. In a recent Rasmussen Poll, 62 percent of surveyed voters listed "education" as a "very important" issue to them—more important than, for example, "immigration," "national security," and "environment."

Almost fifteen years ago, Hoover's Koret Task Force on K–12 Education first appeared on the map as a team with the release of *A Primer on America's Schools*. Part of the volume's purpose was, in the words of Terry M. Moe, the volume's editor, "simply describing and assessing the current state of American education." The task force members did not paint a pretty picture.

In the ensuing decade and a half, much has changed in American education. Charter schools were just a blip on the radar screen; now there are more than five thousand charter schools in the United States with total enrollment approaching two million students. There has been a noticeable change in the demographics of America's children; 61 percent were white in 2000, but by 2010 that number had fallen to 54 percent. (For K–12 public school enrollment, the change is even more dramatic: from 61.2 percent white in 2000 to 52.4 percent white in 2010 to a preliminary estimate of 51.0 percent white in 2013.) Digital learning was more *Jetsons* than *Leave It to Beaver* and, conceptually, was limited primarily to a few science classes at the university level. MOOCs, STEM, Khan Academy, and No Child Left Behind were not in the education lexicon.

Education reform remains necessary because, regrettably, many of the reforms proposed during the past fifteen (some say thirty) years have not worked due to bad design, poor performance, political resistance, or flat-out fear of change. Simply throwing more money at the problem (and K–12 education is a $700 billion industry) has not and, in the task force's view, will not solve our education troubles.

Looking backward with 20/20 hindsight is easy; predicting the future is not, but *planning* for the future is necessary. In this volume, the task force (as it did in 1999–2000) looks at where we've come from but, more important, looks cautiously to the future of American education (as hinted by this book's cover).

There is room for hope, and the task force members express their hope for the future of American education in this volume. Knowing that an educated public is necessary for a free society, we must prepare our children to compete internationally in a highly complex, more technical, global economy. With new technologies, by inculcating a creative educational philosophy, and, at some levels, by breaking from the past, we can prepare our children. In this volume, the task force provides advice for change.

The Hoover Institution strives to generate, nurture, and disseminate ideas defining a free society. Ideas should bloom in the classroom. The intersection of idea-generation at a research center and in the classroom is part of the motivation for the Institution's attention to K–12 education and for the creation of Hoover's Koret Task Force on K–12 Education.

I thank the eleven members of the task force for their work on this book. When the task force first convened in September 1999, today's high school seniors were not yet in kindergarten. Fifteen years later, nine of the eleven original task force members are still with us—a testament to their camaraderie (or resiliency) and to the intellectual stimulation of the task force. I offer special acknowledgment to Chester Finn, the task force chair, and to both Chester and Richard Sousa, who edited this book.

I wish to thank our generous and faithful donors, starting with the Koret Foundation and the Taube Family Foundation and Tad Taube, representing both these philanthropic institutions in their founding and longstanding support for Hoover's education initiative. Other supporters are deserving of acknowledgment for their generosity as well: Lynde and Harry Bradley Foundation, Edmund and Jeannik Littlefield, John M. Olin Foundation, Bernard Lee Schwartz Foundation, Walton Family Foundation, Jack R. and Mary Lois Wheatley, and William E. Simon Foundation. Without their efforts, we would not have accomplished the important and sustaining work over these many years.

For nearly one hundred years, the Hoover Institution has collected rare and at-risk materials for its archives, and our scholars have examined political, economic, and social change. We will continue on that path, developing and marketing *ideas defining a free society*. Nowhere is that more important than in human capital development for our young children. In this volume, Hoover extends its legacy of excellence, producing high-quality scholarship and thoughtful prescriptions for productive policy alternatives.

JOHN RAISIAN
Tad and Dianne Taube Director
Hoover Institution
Stanford, California
January 2014

Introduction

Chester E. Finn Jr.

The coming decade holds immense potential for dramatic improvement in American education and in the achievement of American children—provided that we seize the many opportunities at hand.

But the forces of resistance, lethargy, complacency, and inertia that have largely blocked such dramatic improvements over the past several decades won't magically vanish. Rather, they can be counted upon to do their utmost to keep things pretty much as they have been.

If they again prevail, our standards will remain low, our achievement lacking, our tests not worth preparing students for, our school choices few and often unsatisfactory, our ablest youngsters unchallenged, many of our teachers ill-prepared, our technology just so-so, and our return on investment disappointing. All the while, our many competitors on this shrinking planet will continue to make gains in no small part because the wealthiest and most powerful nation on that planet has failed to maximize its human capital during the period of their lives when girls and boys are most susceptible to learning and when society has the greatest ability to shape what they will learn.

In this volume, members of the Hoover Institution's Koret Task Force on K–12 Education examine both the potentials and the pitfalls that lie ahead for primary-secondary education in the United States.

The eleven of us (plus two emeritus members) have worked together for more than fifteen years to examine, analyze, diagnose, and prescribe for this country's education system across a host of topics. During that time, we have—separately and collectively—authored twenty-one books under the aegis of the task force; we launched (and served as the editorial board for) *Education Next,* today's most significant education-policy journal; we advised governors, legislators, and presidential candidates; we testified at congressional hearings; we met with educators, public officials, and fellow scholars; we took part in innumerable conferences, seminars, and workshops; we wrote countless articles, talked with journalists, and made media appearances; and we deliberated long and hard over an extraordinary array of education-policy issues.

Whew! Although the task force as we have known it will soon change its structure, those issues and the challenges and opportunities that they present are not going away. If anything, they're intensifying.

And so we offer this volume, which mostly looks ahead but does so in the context of where American K–12 education has been, what changes (primarily but not always for the better) have been made, what has and has not been accomplished by way of a comprehensive overhaul, and where things stand today.

As you will see in the eleven short chapters that follow, although far from sanguine, we're fundamentally optimistic about the opportunities at hand. Each task force member tackles one (or a closely related set) of these opportunities. While we cannot claim that the result is completely comprehensive, it's more than illustrative of how our education system could be transformed—and why that's not pie in the sky. We also indicate dozens of ways that further research, policy analysis, and evaluation can assist with (and provide vital feedback on) such a transformation.

The book is organized into three sections.

Part I, *Governance, Politics, and Personnel,* takes up three mega-issues that beset our K–12 system.

Paul Hill considers the ways that the system's inherited structures and governance arrangements get in the way of radical improvement and frames some bold and imaginative alternatives (chapter 1).

Eric Hanushek asks how best to ensure that tomorrow's schools and students have the quality teachers that they need (chapter 2).

Terry Moe examines political obstacles to change, above all teachers unions, and explains how the powerful advance of technology will inexorably weaken their ability to block needed reforms (chapter 3).

Part II, *Crucial Changes,* appraises the current condition of three prominent engines of education reform—standards/assessment/accountability, school choice, and online learning—and sets forth both some challenges that they face and the reasons that those challenges must be overcome.

 John Chubb maps the fast-changing world of online and "blended" learning and shows why, for the first time in memory, even K–12 education will yield—for the better—to improvements made possible by technology (chapter 4).

Herbert Walberg takes stock of school choice in the United States, describing its evolution, what's known about its educational value, and what remains to be investigated (chapter 5).

Williamson Evers takes up the often-contentious realm of academic standards, testing, and accountability with particular reference to the recently developed Common Core standards for English and math and the assessment challenges that accompany them (chapter 6).

Paul Peterson examines a key sub-topic within accountability—holding students themselves responsible for their learning—with particular reference to the hard-to-reform territory of high schools (chapter 7).

Part III, *Resources and Research,* raises four essential concerns about K–12 education and its reform.

Tom Loveless asks how to ensure that our students' future curriculum—buffeted and amplified by new standards, tests, technology, and more—incorporates the most important skills and content and doesn't rekindle yesterday's curriculum wars (chapter 8).

Caroline Hoxby asks whether, in a time of tight budgets, we can afford to make the changes that the system needs—particularly in quality teaching, suitable technology, and sufficient school choices—and shows why the answer is affirmative (chapter 9).

Grover "Russ" Whitehurst asks how we can be confident that our schools and the educational strategies they employ are actually effective and explains how evidence-based research and evaluation can boost that confidence (chapter 10).

And in the final essay, I examine why American education has been neglecting its high-ability (gifted) students and suggest what can be done to develop this vital human resource, both for the country's good and to continue our long march to providing all youngsters with suitable learning opportunities (chapter 11).

My task force colleagues join me in thanking the Hoover Institution for the extraordinary opportunities it has afforded us to meet with, provoke, inform, and advance each other's thinking and stimulate each other's work over the past decade and a half. We thank co-editor (and Hoover's senior associate director) Richard Sousa, who has deftly "herded us cats" with patience, sound judgment, and expert guidance during the entire history of the task force, and Kristen Leffelman, who has helped keep us organized over the past couple of years. We're also deeply grateful to the Koret Foundation and other generous donors to Hoover that have made all this possible.

The task force's combined activities may be winding down. But we are not—and we look forward to continuing our quest to bring scholarship, analysis, and forthrightness to bear on the challenges and opportunities that face American education in the years ahead.

List of Acronyms

AFT	American Federation of Teachers
AP	Advanced Placement
CCSSI	Common Core State Standards Initiative
CCSSO	Council of Chief State School Officers
ELA	English Language Arts
ETS	Education Testing Service
FCAT	Florida Comprehensive Assessment Test
IES	Institute of Education Sciences
IU	Intermediate Education Unit
K–12	Kindergarten through 12th Grade
KIPP	Knowledge Is Power Program
LIFO	Last in, first out
MOOC	Massive Open Online Course
NAEP	National Assessment of Educational Progress
NCLB	No Child Left Behind
NCTM	National Council of Teachers of Mathematics
NEA	National Education Association
NGA	National Governors Association
NSF	National Science Foundation
OECD	Organisation for Economic Co-operation and Development
PISA	Programme for International Student Assessment
RttT	Race to the Top
STEM	Science, Technology, Engineering, and Mathematics
TIMSS	Trends in International Mathematics and Science Study
VOISE	Virtual Opportunities Inside a School Environment
WWC	What Works Clearinghouse

Part I: Governance, Politics, and Personnel

Rethinking Governance

Boosting Teacher Effectiveness

Facing the Union Challenge

CHAPTER 1

Rethinking Governance

Paul T. Hill

The Real Impact of Governance in Public Education

Is talk of governance a distraction in the effort to improve America's schools? Some people claim so. Children don't learn from elected officials or the laws and regulations they create; students learn from teachers. Just give every child a good teacher, some say, and all the problems of our schools would be solved. They would be right, of course, if only it were possible to give every child a better teacher without changing the rules by which public schools are governed.

Governance—the rules made by school boards, legislatures, and bureaucracies, and the actions those bodies take to make sure the rules are followed—ultimately determines who teaches whom and what gets taught. Governance sets teacher pay scales and licensing standards. Collective bargaining agreements are part of governance, and they control how teachers are hired, assigned to schools, assigned work, and evaluated. Governance also determines what schools teach, how they use time and money, how their performance is judged, and whether anything is done about a school where children are not learning.

Public education requires governance because it involves two takings of liberty: taxpayers are compelled to pay for it, and parents are compelled either to send their children to publicly funded schools or to make other arrangements at their own expense. Publicly funded education is the only realistic option for the vast majority of parents.

Important conflicts are inherent to public education. Conflicts are found among the preferences of policymakers who define the purposes of public education, the taxpayers who pay for it, parents who surrender their children to it, and educators who are paid to deliver it. These conflicts can never be fully resolved, but they can be managed via agreements about rules and processes for making decisions and managing what gets done. Thus the need for governance.

The Harm Done by Current Governance Arrangements

Public education governance in the United States is a weird product of our nation's history, federal structure, and openness to political entrepreneurship. Nobody designed our mishmash of governance arrangements. Instead, they arose a little bit at a time in response to crises, political entrepreneurship, and interest-group opportunism.

Due to our frontier past, schools grew organically in individual towns and neighborhoods, long before state governments seriously took on the responsibility for education assigned to them by their constitutions. Once states started regulating and funding K–12 education, tensions about who was in charge began. The national government, long inactive in K–12 education, burst into action during the 1960s War on Poverty. Its programs and carrot-and-stick approach (subsidies in return for mandated activities) created new regulatory pressures on schools. Our history of school segregation ultimately pulled courts into K–12. Once the courts proved willing to rule on a broad range of issues framed around equal protection of the laws, they too became sources of rules and constraints, sometimes at odds with those created by other units of government. In the 1970s teachers unions became the dominant organized force in public education; negotiated collective bargaining agreements became the most potent source of constraints on how teachers work and schools operate.

As a result, K–12 governance is chaotic. Every level of government imposes controls of some kind on how funds will be used and accounted for, who may teach, what jobs teachers may and may not do, how many students may be assigned to a teacher in an hour or a day, what hours and days schools will operate, how space and equipment will be used, what parent groups must be consulted before decisions are made, what facilities schools may occupy, etc.[1] School boards can intervene in almost any detail of school operation under the guise of casework for constituents.[2] Teachers' collective bargaining agreements, court orders, and individualized education plans for students with special needs are also part of governance. So are licensing policies that exclude many people with relevant skills from working in schools.

Governance can tie up funds on unproductive activities, causing schools to spend more for facilities and transportation than school leaders would do if they had their choice, or to teach some students courses they are not prepared for and to teach other students subjects they already know.

Our system acts as if the exercise of discretion and the expertise that goes along with it are dangerous. Over time, as problems arise and new rules are created in an (often futile) effort to ensure that they never happen again, constraints on the educators and parents grow.

Today's governance makes it difficult for the people who know what children need to act on what they know. Parents who know what their children need are given few options to choose the school that best fits their children's needs; principals who have the skills and attitudes to identify a teacher who can be effective in a particular context are denied the opportunity to do so; teachers and school leaders who know the school's needs and therefore how it should spend its budget are prevented from doing so; and teachers who know what their students have and haven't mastered are denied the discretion that would enable them to use such knowledge to develop a new curriculum or engage technology to help.

Can We Get Governance Right?

How to fix public education governance in the United States is not a new question. Analysts have suggested many alternative forms of governance, each intended to shift the locus of decision-making from local school boards and state legislatures to other entities, including mayors, parents, and school entrepreneurs.

Milton Friedman's book *Capitalism and Freedom* set off a debate on education governance that continues to this day. He argued for putting parents in charge. John Chubb and Terry Moe suggested a more complex system, with parents in charge but also some roles for regulators, from whom school operators would need to get licenses.[3] Moe has since made a strong case for a mixed system in which government's role is strictly limited and choice and entrepreneurship are emphasized.[4]

Others have suggested leaving a government-operated school system intact, but putting different people—mayors,[5] appointed boards, or state officials[6]—in charge and using performance standards to focus the attention of educators on student learning, not distracting rules.[7]

Proposals to fix governance by putting mayors or state officials in charge are popular, if poorly thought-through. A change in mode of selection is always a good idea when a governing body is overly politicized or deadlocked.[8]

Takeovers by mayors have overcome the blocking power of unions and district bureaucracies in New York, Hartford, Connecticut, and other cities, but they only work for a while. The same is true of takeovers by special masters or statewide school districts like Louisiana's Recovery School District. As this is written, the New York and Hartford reforms are both in danger of being thrown out by successor mayors who can gain union support by bashing their predecessors' policies. The promising state takeover in Oakland, California, has already been abandoned under political pressure. Louisiana's Recovery District is required by law to return schools to local control.

Mayorally appointed boards and superintendents can run into the same problems as elected ones, particularly if provider groups or political machines control appointments. Appointed boards often confound the expectations of mayors and others who appoint them, just as elected boards can disappoint voters. Any way of selecting board members is open to abuse. When things are not working out well under one method, the grass can look much greener under another.

More fundamental new governance ideas from both sides of the political spectrum also have flaws, from even more open town-meeting style control of schools on the left to total abandonment of governance in preference for market mechanisms on the right.

Unbounded public deliberation about the goals and means of public education would lead to continual and escalating regulation of schools, accelerating the harmful developments of the past thirty years. Each succeeding crisis or emergence of a noble cause would lead to new regulations, to be layered on top of those created earlier.

In an ideal world, well-intentioned regulation driven by community politics would serve to increase equity of access and outcomes. In practice, it leads to precisely the opposite outcome by severing the link between those who know something that might help and those who make the decisions.

Total reliance on the market is also unrealistic. A pure market would allow only parents' consumer behavior to govern who ran schools, which schools were forced to close, what schools offered in the way of instruction, and thus ultimately what children would learn. While consumer choice would drive improvement, it is likely that, absent government oversight, data-cooking and exclusion of hard-to-educate students by a subset of schools would destabilize the entire arrangement.[9] Our existing legal protections governing discrimination and child protection would lead to court intervention and piecemeal re-regulation of exactly the kind that produced the irrational governance system we have today.

A pure market would in time attract innovators and entrepreneurs with new ideas about how to meet existing and new needs. It would also ultimately teach families the consequences of bad choices—as poorly prepared children could not get needed education or jobs—but nobody knows whether that would take a few years or a few generations.[10] In the meantime, many could suffer, and the pressure for re-regulation would be hard to resist.

Governance changes are tricky. Proposals that assume that some class of actors, if put fully in charge, will naturally seek effective schools for all children are doomed to failure. No one group or entity has exactly the same interest as children, and each can be expected, in the long run, to pull schooling, and the uses of public funds, in directions that meet its own interests.

Proposals that educators be left to govern themselves, deciding how much money schools need and assessing their own performance, are obvious non-starters. Teachers have their own interests and can't always be trusted to automatically give children what they need. Similarly, proposals that governance be reduced to standard-setting are based on the Pollyanna assumption that lack of knowledge about what students need to know is the only barrier to effective, concerted action among educators, parents, and taxpayers. Misalignment in the education system is due to differences in agendas and interests, not to lack of information.

Proposals that charter schools or charter management organizations should govern themselves constrained only by family choices are similarly naïve. Charter school operators have very good motives—to serve the students they enroll as effectively as possible—but they are not responsible for any student they do not admit. Predictably, some charter operators in New Orleans have tried to avoid serving disabled children, and some charters in New York City have tried to rig admissions lotteries and have refused to admit children who move into the city in the middle of the school year. Online education providers in Ohio have worked hard to prevent competitors from entering the marketplace.

Only a few charter schools and online providers have done these things. Nor will most public school teachers cheat their students by tampering with test booklets to inflate the results. But such things do happen because some actors will define their interests narrowly. Because one dramatic case of neglect or discrimination can lead to re-regulation, a stable governance system cannot place blind trust in any group.

Emerging "Mixed Governance" Ideas

It is possible to move toward a system that harnesses the power of markets by significantly enhancing the openness and competitiveness of the system and choice for families while at the same time creating real protections for children who might otherwise suffer discrimination and neglect.

Since 1990, promising new ideas about limiting governance and employing market mechanisms have emerged. Led by Chubb and Moe in *Politics, Markets, and America's Schools*,[11] these proposals would limit government to oversight rather than operation of public schools. Independent parties would operate schools, choose curricula and instructional approaches, employ staff, and control budgets based on student enrollment.[12] Parents would freely choose any school. Government would only license, contract with, or charter schools and ensure that parents had access to good performance information.

The most recent "constitutional" proposal is the most explicit: local school boards should have no powers whatever other than to decide on a slate of independently run schools to operate in their localities.[13] By law, school boards would be forbidden to employ teachers or principals, incur debts, or own property. Schools could enforce their freedom from regulation in court.

Growing numbers of states and localities are experimenting with one or another of these proposals, all of which are consistent with the principle expressed by David Osborne and Ted Gaebler that "government should steer but not row."[14] Some states' movement from program-based to pupil-based funding and investment in longitudinal student performance databases reinforce these developments in governance.

In the next ten years, ideas like these will need to be tried and refined to make room for new possibilities created by technology and social entrepreneurship:

- Schools that serve students statewide or even nationally, via online instruction

- Hybrid schools where student and teacher work is organized around individualized, computer-based learning, which might employ fewer but more highly skilled teachers, require student attendance only part-time, and need far more modest facilities than existing schools

- Schools that don't employ teachers directly but obtain them from specialized services (analogous to providers of specialized physician services to hospitals)

- Voucher systems that allow parents to hire different providers for different parts of their child's learning experiences

To accommodate these inevitable changes in educational practice and instructional delivery, governance must become less bound to geographically defined provision; less prescriptive about whom schools employ and how they use time and money; more focused on accountability for performance; and vastly less focused on compliance. Yet, voters will still demand accounting for public funds and evidence of results. Courts and legislatures can't be prevented from taking action when someone can make a good case that children have been neglected or abused.

The Work of the Next Decade

Governance challenges are not insoluble. But solving them requires hard thinking about design, disciplined experimentation with possible solutions, and close analysis of real-world experience. Any governance reform must be closely scrutinized for its susceptibility to "capture," i.e., one group's domination of schools in its own interest.

There will be no substitute for data-based tracking of implementation, results, and unexpected developments. Things seldom work out as intended, both because theorists who invent new governance ideas can seldom think through all the angles the first time and because good ideas can be distorted in implementation.

Failure to track implementation can mean a governance idea is called a proven failure when in fact it was never tried. In Philadelphia, for example, opponents claimed that increasing school-level control of resources was a failure because student results did not improve. Reformers had no response to these claims, though subsequent analysis showed that the schools concerned never got the promised freedom over staffing and spending and that the traditional schools to which they were compared got a great deal of extra money.

Solving the governance problem will require serious analysis, not just sloganeering. When it comes to creating a governance system in which schools are free from continual re-regulation, the truth sounds paradoxical: schools would be freer and suffer less governance instability if new governance plans anticipated areas in which schools would surely be regulated and were clear about what data and other forms of evidence schools must provide.

Notes

1. For extensive critiques of existing governance arrangements, see Noel Epstein, *Who's In Charge Here? The Tangled Web of School Governance and Policy* (Washington, DC: Brookings Institution Press, 2004). See also Dominic Brewer and Joanna Smith, "Evaluating the 'Crazy Quilt': Educational Governance in California" (Stanford, CA: Institute for Research on Education Policy and Practice, 2006).

2. For a review of school board duties as assigned by state legislation, see Paul T. Hill, Christine Campbell, Kelly Warner-King, Meaghan McElroy, and Isabel Munoz-Colon, "Big City School Boards: Problems and Options" (Seattle: Center on Reinventing Public Education, 2003).

3. John Chubb and Terry M. Moe, *Politics, Markets, and America's Schools* (Washington, DC: Brookings Institution Press, 1990).

4. Terry M. Moe and Paul T. Hill, "Moving to a Mixed Model: Without an Appropriate Role for the Market, the Education Sector Will Stagnate," in *The Futures of School Reform*, ed. Jal Mehta, Robert B. Schwartz, and Frederick M. Hess (Cambridge, MA: Harvard Education Press, 2012).

5. Kenneth K. Wong, Francis X. Shen, Dorothea Anagnostopoulos, and Stacey Rutledge, *The Education Mayor: Improving America's Schools* (Washington, DC: Georgetown University Press, 2007). See also Kenneth K. Wong, "Measuring the Effectiveness of Mayoral Takeover as a School Reform Strategy," *Peabody Journal of Education* 78, no. 4 (2003): 89–119.

6. Chester E. Finn Jr., "Reinventing Local Control," *Education Week*, January 23, 1991, 40.

7. Jennifer A. O'Day and Marshall S. Smith, "Systemic Reform and Educational Opportunity," in *Designing Coherent Education Policy: Improving the System*, ed. Susan H. Fuhrman (San Francisco: Jossey-Bass, 1993), 250–312.

8. Ashley Jochim and Paul T. Hill, "Mayoral Intervention: Right for Seattle Schools?" (Seattle: Center on Reinventing Public Education, 2008).

9. Cases brought by parents of handicapped children already threaten re-regulation of the all-charter New Orleans public school system.

10. On the time dimension in implementation of choice, see a recent Hoover Institution Press book by the present author, *Learning as We Go: Why School Choice is Worth the Wait* (2010).

11. Chubb and Moe, *Politics, Markets, and America's Schools*.

12. See, for example, Paul T. Hill, Lawrence Pierce, and James Guthrie, *Reinventing Public Education: How Contracting Can Transform America's Schools* (Chicago: University of Chicago Press, 1997); Andy Smarick, *The Urban School System of the Future: Applying the Principles and Lessons of Chartering* (Lanham, MD: Rowman and Littlefield, 2012); Paul T. Hill, Christine Campbell, and Betheny Gross, *Strife and Progress: Portfolio Strategies to Manage Urban Schools* (Washington, DC: Brookings Institution Press, 2012); and Neerav Kingsland, "An Open Letter to Urban Superintendents in the United States of America, Part I: Reformers and Relinquishers," in *Rick Hess Straight Up* (blog), January 23, 2012, http://blogs.edweek.org /edweek/rick_hess_straight_up/2012/01/an_open_letter _to_urban_superintendents_in_the_united_states_of _america.html; and William Guenther and Justin Cohen, *Smart Districts: Restructuring Urban Systems from the School Up* (Boston: Mass Insight, 2012).

13. Paul T. Hill, "Picturing a Different Governance Structure for Public Education," in *Education Governance for the Twenty-first Century: Overcoming the Structural Barriers to School Reform*, ed. Patrick McGuinn and Paul Manna (Washington, DC: Brookings Institution Press, 2013).

14. David Osborne and Ted Gaebler, *Reinventing Government: How the Entrepreneurial Spirit is Transforming the Public Sector* (Reading, MA: Addison-Wesley, 1992).

CHAPTER 2

Boosting Teacher Effectiveness

Eric A. Hanushek

Over the last two decades, research on student achievement has pinpointed the central role of teachers. While other factors—families, peers, neighborhoods—are obviously elements in a student's learning, it is the school and particularly the teachers and administrators who are given the public responsibility for the education of our youth. There is a general consensus that improving the effectiveness of teachers is the key to lifting student achievement, although questions remain about how best to do this.

A key element in focusing attention on the importance of teacher effectiveness was research that took an outcomes-based perspective.[1] By looking at differences in the growth of student achievement across different teachers instead of concentrating on just the background and characteristics of teachers, it was possible to identify the true impact of teachers on students. This work, now generally called value-added analysis, demonstrated that some teachers consistently get greater learning gains year after year than other teachers. In fact, the average learning gains associated with a teacher provide a convenient metric for teacher effectiveness.

We now have a substantial number of studies that indicate clearly how much difference teacher effectiveness makes to student outcomes. In one study of mine, teachers near the top of the quality distribution got an entire year's worth of additional learning out of their students compared to those near the bottom.[2] That is, a good teacher will get a gain of 1.5 grade level equivalents while a bad teacher will get 0.5 year during a single academic year. Importantly, this analysis considered kids just from minority and poor inner-city families, indicating that family background is not fate and that good teachers can overcome deficits that might come from poorer learning conditions in the home.

A second perspective comes from combining existing quantitative estimates of how differences in teacher quality relate to achievement gaps by race or income.[3] Moving from an average teacher to one at the eighty-fourth percentile of teacher quality (i.e., moving up one standard deviation in teacher quality) would close somewhere between one-quarter and one-third of the average gap in math achievement between kids eligible for free and reduced-price lunches and those with higher incomes. Said differently, having a good teacher as opposed to an average teacher for three to four years in a row would, by available estimates, close the achievement gap by income. Closing the black-white achievement gap, which is a little larger than the average income gap, would take good teachers three and a half to five years in a row.

Perhaps the most valuable way to see differences for the subsequent discussion of salaries is to calculate the impacts of effective teachers on the future earnings of students.[4] A teacher who raises the achievement of a student will tend, other things being equal, to raise earnings throughout that student's work life. We can in fact calculate the economic impact on the student from analyses of how achievement translates into higher incomes. Using 2010 earnings, for example, a teacher in the seventy-fifth percentile would on average raise each student's lifetime income by somewhat

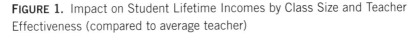

FIGURE 1. Impact on Student Lifetime Incomes by Class Size and Teacher Effectiveness (compared to average teacher)

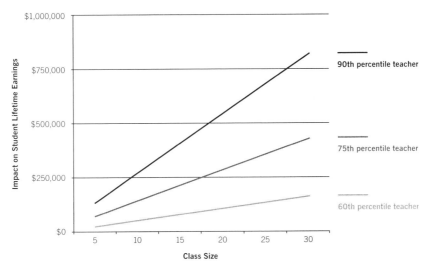

more than $14,300 when compared to the average teacher. (All calculations are based on present values at the time of high school graduation where future incomes are discounted at 3 percent per year). But, this is not fully what the seventy-fifth percentile teacher contributes, because each student in the class can expect the same enhanced income. Thus, with a class of twenty-five students, this teacher would add $358,000 in future income compared to an average teacher.

Figure 1 shows the total contribution of teachers at the sixtieth, seventy-fifth, and ninetieth percentile of teacher effectiveness with varying class sizes. Excellent teachers add over $800,000 to the future incomes of students in a class of thirty. Even a teacher just above average at the sixtieth percentile would add over $100,000 to a class of twenty students.

These are calculations for each school year. Each and every year throughout their careers that these above-average teachers are teaching adds hundreds of thousands of dollars to their students' future incomes. They also parallel a recent set of direct estimates of income effects that comes from linking teacher "value-added" to income tax records.[5]

But, there is the darker side. Below-average teachers are subtracting from student earnings at a similar rate. The tenth percentile teacher, compared to an average teacher, subtracts over a half million dollars per year for each twenty students he or she teaches. For the tenth, twenty-fifth, and fortieth percentile teacher, one simply has to put a minus sign in front of the values seen in figure 1.

From these different perspectives, the answer is the same: teachers have an enormous influence on students and on their futures.

Of course, there are two ways to look at the policy relevance of these figures. One is to assume that the current stock of teachers is fixed so that it is all just a zero-sum game—what one student gains, another student loses by being stuck with a below-average teacher. In such a case teacher policy would amount to deciding one way or another who gets the good teachers and who gets the bad teachers. It could, for example, be decided by market forces that allocate teachers to schools, or it could be decided by regulatory approaches, perhaps emanating from court cases and the like.

When viewed as just a distributional issue, the country as a whole would be no better off in terms of overall productivity by potential policy changes (even if the outcomes were viewed as more just). This result is not consistent with the primary concerns about education that relate to the overall productivity and output of the nation.

The second way to look at the prior calculations is more consistent with our investment notions about education. The impact of teachers on lifetime earnings is meant to signal how the productivity of individuals changes with different skills. The figures indicate the gains that would accrue to having more teachers of the type found in the top of the current effectiveness distribution. Similarly, they indicate the gains that would accrue to having fewer teachers near the bottom of the current distribution. In other words, a policy that increased the average quality of the teacher distribution from that currently in place would yield potentially large overall gains to the economy (and potentially improve distributional matters at the same time).

To illustrate this, I have used the information available about the varying effectiveness of the teacher force to understand the aggregate impact of policies aimed at eliminating the worst teachers (an issue with direct policy implications as discussed below). I have projected the achievement impact of replacing varying percentages of the bottom teachers with average teachers.[6] By eliminating just the bottom 5–8 percent of teachers, the available research suggests that US achievement could climb to the level of Canadian achievement (as measured by international assessments of math and science).

Paul E. Peterson, Ludger Woessmann, and I have developed the economic implications of improving achievement to the level of Canada.[7] This analysis is based on the strong impacts of worker skills on future economic growth. It suggests that all workers in the United States could, by historical results, expect an average increase in their paychecks of 20 percent for each of the next eighty years. An alternative way to look at this is that the current fiscal problems could be readily solved by improved education that led to improved growth. Clearly, similar to the individual findings, there are substantial economic gains that seem apparent from policies that upgrade the quality of teachers.

While less well-developed, an increasing body of evidence points to the importance of principal quality.[8] The currently available research, based on the value added by a principal to achievement of students in the school, indicates that the principal may have an impact on achievement similar to that of teachers, although the principal affects the entire school.

Current Policy Discussions

Policy debates have changed swiftly to incorporate the research evidence on teachers.[9] It is difficult to enter into any school policy discussion that does not touch on the issue of teacher quality.

Moreover, the character of the discussions has become much more sophisticated and knowledgeable. The naïve calls for "highly qualified teachers" in the No Child Left Behind act have been replaced by recognition that credentials and qualifications—the objects of past policies—are not closely related to teacher effectiveness in the classroom. While there has been no rush to eliminate salary differentials based on advanced degrees (about 10 percent of all teacher salary payments), they have become a greater part of the discussion.

Similarly, a teacher's classroom experience after the first few years has been shown to have no effect on teacher performance. There has been little discussion of eliminating the longevity portion of teachers' salaries, even though over one-quarter of the total wage bill goes to bonuses for teachers with greater than two years of experience (around the cutoff in the evidence about the returns to experience). But there has been intense discussion of LIFO provisions—last in, first out—in laws and contracts that govern separations during force reductions. These policies are closely related to the evidence on effectiveness and experience. The use of LIFO rules instead of ones based on teacher effectiveness have been shown to increase the number of teachers who must be dismissed and to dramatically alter the quality of dismissals when compared to policies based on effectiveness.[10]

While considerable discussion exists on how we might want to change schools of education, little of this is directly related to the performance of students. Indeed, we have just rudimentary evidence on whether some schools of education do a better job than others. There is suggestive information in the fact that there is not very much difference in average effectiveness by teachers' routes into their careers (certified vs. non-certified).[11]

Similarly, many would like to use improved professional development to upgrade the teaching force, but many questions about the efficacy of this remain.[12] Further (scientific) research on the issues surrounding professional development could prove helpful in deciding the overall thrust of teacher improvement policies.

Importantly, with the recognition of the importance of teacher quality has come a new interest in how labor laws and teacher contracts affect student outcomes.[13] The turmoil in Wisconsin got the most attention as the state limited bargaining to just wages and benefits and removed larger issues such as class sizes and teacher assignment policies. Partly because of Wisconsin and partly on their own, a number of other states entered into active discussions of state restrictions on teaching.

A central part of much of the teacher quality discussion has been the use of value-added measures of quality. The value-added measures are designed to provide estimates of the independent effect of the teacher on the growth in a student's learning and to separate this from other influences on achievement such as families, peers, and neighborhoods. The validity and reliability of these measures have been widely debated and are the subject of considerable current research.[14]

The discussions range across a number of statistical and policy issues. But the discussion was accelerated when the *Los Angeles Times* and the *New York Times* (among others) published the names and value-added rankings of thousands of local teachers. The public attention to variations in teacher effectiveness led to an uproar—an uproar that helped focus the policy discussion and local bargaining.

Attention to test scores in the value-added estimation raises issues of the narrowness of the tests, of the limited numbers of teachers in tested subjects and grades, of the accuracy of linking teachers and students, and of the measurement errors in the achievement tests. Each is an important issue that has fueled continuing research efforts. This subsequent research is helping to define how best to use the statistical evidence on teacher quality.

The value-added discussions have also opened new consideration of alternative ways of valuing teachers. While teachers have always been evaluated in some manner, it is clear that until recently the evaluations provided little information, particularly for making any personnel decisions.[15] Thus, efforts have been made to develop and use observational protocols that more accurately indicate classroom effectiveness.[16]

A closely related discussion has revolved around the use of performance pay. Teachers are currently paid according to experience and to possession of an advanced degree, neither of which is closely related to classroom effectiveness. The argument has long been made that at least a portion of pay should reflect merit in order to provide incentives for teachers to do better. This idea led to a somewhat ill-conceived experiment by Vanderbilt researchers in which a randomly selected group of teachers received bonuses based on the performance of their students.[17] When compared to students of teachers not receiving any bonuses, students of those with the possibility of performance pay did no better. This study demonstrated that offering a bonus for better performance to existing teachers has very little influence on what they do. This is exactly what has been shown by the multiple studies of merit pay that focus on the impact of relatively small bonuses for current teachers on their performance in the classroom. The simplest interpretation is that almost all current teachers are indeed working to do the best that they can.

At the same time, this is not a demonstration that salaries have no effect. Both the level of salaries and the pattern of salaries across teachers affect who enters and who stays in teaching. Higher salaries and a greater relationship to performance would attract a different group of people into teaching. Indeed, the impact of salaries on selection into teaching is the key issue for those who think that performance pay is important.

Nonetheless, the availability of this "gold standard" study has allowed the unions and the schools to argue that performance pay has been tried and simply has not worked. This situation actually demonstrates a further issue in making evidenced-based policy. It is often possible to find or to interpret evidence in order to support very different positions. This in fact has made moving to rational policy positions more difficult, particularly in areas of personnel policy where vested interests are especially important.

The possibility of evidence being hijacked for the use of special interest groups serves to reinforce the need for continued research and evaluation. Only superior and more reliable evidence can top the biased use of evidence.

The Prospects for Further Improvement

The world of education is moving steadily toward reliance on evidence, even with the possibility for misinterpretation. Moreover, the evidence on teacher quality issues is beginning to win the day.

The movement toward better overall policy is seen directly in state actions. For example, all states except California had unique student identifiers in 2011; thirty-five had unique teacher identifiers that allowed linking teachers to students.[18] Between 2009 and 2011, twenty-six states moved to include evidence of student learning in teacher evaluations, and ten states mandated that student learning would be the preponderant criterion in local evaluations.

In teacher tenure decisions, there has been considerable recent progress. More and more states are moving to require evidence of teacher effectiveness and to extend the minimum number of years for tenure. About a third of states also support differential pay in shortage subject areas and do not have regulatory language blocking differential pay. Similarly, about a third of states support differentially rewarding effective teachers.

While there is a considerable way to go in expanding and refining these changes, the pattern of state policies toward effective teachers has changed dramatically in recent years.

And there is a new sense of forward movement at the local level. Perhaps the best story comes from Washington, DC. This district, by far the worst in the nation, went through agonizing battles between Michelle Rhee (the former chancellor of Washington public schools) and the unions. But four years ago the unions agreed to a new contract that introduced both value-added and observational evaluations and that used them in personnel decisions. At this time about one thousand teachers have received substantial increases in their base salaries because of continued top performance. But close to 500 teachers have been dismissed because of continued poor performance. The whole evaluation system is continually being developed and improved, but it has reached a level of acceptance that bodes well for the future.

Importantly, there is now direct evidence that the Washington, DC, personnel policies are paying off. Thomas Dee and James Wyckoff found that dismissal threats increased the voluntary attrition of low-performing teachers by more than 50 percent.[19] Additionally, low-performing teachers who stayed improved their performance significantly, as did high-performing teachers who were in the range to get bonuses.

Similarly, the Los Angeles Unified School District has moved to remove around one hundred poorly performing teachers. While this remains small compared to the total number of teachers in Los Angeles, it is orders of magnitude larger than what was seen just a couple of years ago.

Many states and localities are developing what must be thought of as experimental programs for ensuring teacher quality. The key to the future is validating and replicating the ones that prove successful and eliminating the ones that do not. Doing this requires a strong research and evaluation activity to match the policy experimentation.

Notes

1. Eric A. Hanushek, "Teacher Characteristics and Gains in Student Achievement: Estimation Using Micro-Data," *American Economic Review* 60, no. 2 (May 1971): 280–288.

2. Eric A. Hanushek, "The Trade-Off Between Child Quantity and Quality," *Journal of Political Economy* 100, no. 1 (February 1992): 84–117.

3. Eric A. Hanushek and Steven G. Rivkin, "The Distribution of Teacher Quality and Implications for Policy," *Annual Review of Economics* 4 (2012): 131–157.

4. Eric A. Hanushek, "Valuing Teachers: How Much is a Good Teacher Worth?" *Education Next* 11, no. 3 (Summer 2011).

5. Raj Chetty, John N. Friedman, and Jonah E. Rockoff, "The Long-Term Impacts of Teachers: Teacher Value-Added and Student Outcomes in Adulthood" (NBER working paper 17699, Cambridge, MA: National Bureau of Economic Research, December 2011).

6. Eric A. Hanushek, "The Economic Value of Higher Teacher Quality," *Economics of Education Review* 30, no. 3 (June 2011): 466–479.

7. Eric A. Hanushek, Paul E. Peterson, and Ludger Woessmann, *Endangering Prosperity: A Global View of the American School* (Washington, DC: Brookings Institution Press, 2013).

8. Gregory F. Branch, Eric A. Hanushek, and Steven G. Rivkin, "School Leaders Matter: Measuring the impact of Effective Principals," *Education Next* 13, no. 1 (Winter 2013): 62–69.

9. For example, John E. Chubb, *The Best Teachers in the World: Why We Don't Have Them and How We Could* (Stanford, CA: Hoover Institution Press, 2012).

10. For example, Donald Boyd, Hamilton Lankford, Susanna Loeb, and James Wyckoff, "Teacher Layoffs: An Empirical Illustration of Seniority versus Measures of Effectiveness," *Education Finance and Policy* 6, no. 3 (Summer 2011): 439–454.

11. For example, Thomas J. Kane, Jonah E. Rockoff, and Douglas O. Staiger, "What Does Certification Tell Us About Teacher

Effectiveness? Evidence from New York City," *Economics of Education Review* 27, no. 6 (December 2008): 615–631; and Donald J. Boyd, Pamela L. Grossman, Hamilton Lankford, Susanna Loeb, and James Wyckoff, "Teacher Preparation and Student Achievement," *Educational Evaluation and Policy Analysis* 31, no. 4 (December 2009): 416–440.

12. For example, Michael S. Garet, Stephanie Cronen, Marian Eaton, Anja Kurki, Meredith Ludwig, Wehmah Jones, Kazuaki Uekawa, Audrey Falk, Howard S. Bloom, Fred Doolittle, Pei Zhu, and Laura Sztejnberg, "The Impact of Two Professional Development Interventions on Early Reading Instruction and Achievement," National Center for Education Evaluation and Regional Assistance, Institute of Education Sciences (Washington, DC: US Department of Education, September 2009); and Michael S. Garet, Andrew J. Wayne, Fran Stancavage, James Taylor, Marian Eaton, Kirk Walters, Mengli Song, Seth Brown, Steven Hurlburt, Pei Zhu, Susan Sepanik, and Fred Doolittle, "Middle School Mathematics Professional Development Impact Study: Findings After the Second Year of Implementation," NCEE 2011-4024 (Washington, DC: Institute of Education Sciences, April 2011).

13. Terry M. Moe, *Special Interest: Teachers Unions and America's Public Schools* (Washington, DC: Brookings Institution Press, 2011).

14. Steven Glazerman, Susanna Loeb, Dan Goldhaber, Douglas Staiger, Stephen Raudenbush, and Grover Whitehurst, "Evaluating Teachers: The Important Role of Value-Added," The Brookings Brown Center Task Group on Teacher Quality (Washington, DC: Brookings Institution Press, November 17, 2010).

15. For example, Daniel Weisberg, Susan Sexton, Jennifer Mulhern, and David Keeling, "The Widget Effect: Our National Failure to Acknowledge and Act on Differences in Teacher Effectiveness," 2nd ed. (New York: The New Teacher Project, 2009).

16. Thomas J. Kane, Daniel F. McCaffrey, Trey Miller, and Douglas O. Staiger, "Have We Identified Effective Teachers? Validating Measures of Effective Teaching Using Random Assignment," Measures of Effective Teaching project, Bill and Melinda Gates Foundation (January 2013).

17. Matthew G. Springer, Dale Ballou, Laura Hamilton, Vi-Nhuan Le, J.R. Lockwood, Daniel F. McCaffrey, Matthew Pepper, and Brian M. Stecher, "Teacher Pay for Performance: Experimental Evidence from the Project on Incentives in Teaching" (Nashville, TN: National Center on Performance Incentives, Vanderbilt University, 2010).

18. National Council on Teacher Quality, "State Teacher Policy Yearbook, 2011" (Washington, DC: National Council on Teacher Quality, 2012).

19. Thomas Dee and James Wyckoff, "Incentives, Selection, and Teacher Performance: Evidence from IMPACT" (NBER Working paper WP19529, Cambridge, MA: National Bureau of Economic Research, October 2013).

CHAPTER 3

Facing the Union Challenge

Terry M. Moe

Since *A Nation at Risk* warned in 1983 of a "rising tide of medi-ocrity" in America's schools, the nation has invested heavily in reform efforts to bring about significant improvement—generating countless changes to the laws, programs, structures, and curricula of public education, and spending untold billions of extra dollars.[1] All this activity might seem to be the sign of a well-functioning democracy. But pull away the curtain and the picture is not nearly so pretty: the reforms of the last few decades, despite all the fan-fare, have been incremental and weak in practice. The nation is constantly busy with education reforms not because it is responsi-bly addressing social problems, but because it never actually solves them and they never go away—leading to continuing demands for *more* reforms. This is what keeps the "education reform era" alive and kicking: not democracy, not responsibility, but failure.

The reasons for this failure can be as complex as we want to make them. But the fact is, in American education—and most areas of public policy, for that matter—there are simple fundamen-tals at work that go a long way toward explaining the obstacles

to major institutional change. The most important is the power
of vested interests. In the American public school system, the key
vested interests are the teachers unions: the National Education
Association, the American Federation of Teachers, and their state
and local affiliates, which represent the system's key employees and
are by far the most powerful groups in the politics of education.
Major reform is threatening to their vested interests in the existing system, and they have used their formidable power to repel and
weaken the efforts of reformers to bring real change. This is not the
whole story of the modern reform era, needless to say. But it is at
the heart of it.[2]

Fortunately, for reasons I will explain, the prospects for change
are much brighter in the decades ahead. And there are actions that
policymakers and researchers can take that will pave the way and
help bring that change earlier rather than later.

Collective Bargaining and Ineffective Organization

As House Speaker Tip O'Neill famously noted, all politics is local.
And so it is with the teachers unions. It is their locals that attract
the members, money, and activists that are the ingredients of union
power in politics. Their ability to attract these resources is aided
immensely by collective bargaining, for this is what teachers care
most about as union members and it is what ties them securely to
their unions.[3]

Collective bargaining is also profoundly important for another
reason: it has enabled the unions to impose ineffective forms of
organization on the schools, thus exacerbating the very problems
the reform movement has been trying to correct. Among other
things, local contract provisions tend to include salary rules that
pay teachers based on seniority and formal credits with no attention to performance; seniority rules for transfers and layoffs that
allow senior teachers to lay claim to available jobs; and onerous

rules for evaluation and dismissal that virtually assure that all teachers will get satisfactory evaluations and no one will be dismissed for poor performance.

These and countless other contract rules are designed to promote the job-related interests of teachers, but from the standpoint of effective organization they are simply perverse.[4] Yet this is how America's schools are actually organized. There is a disconnect between what the public schools are supposed to do and how they are organized to do it—and this disconnect is a built-in feature of the modern American school system, a reflection of its underlying structure of power.

Why have the districts "agreed" to ineffective organization? Partly it's because no district wants a fight, because most work rules don't cost them anything and because as monopolies they have had little incentive historically to insist on effective organization anyway. But there is also a crucial *political* reason: school board members are elected, and the teachers unions are typically the most powerful forces in those local elections. As a result, many board members are union allies, others are reliably sympathetic to collective bargaining, and the rest have reason to fear that, if they cross the unions, their jobs are at stake.[5]

Over the last decade, districts have had their spines stiffened a bit by the achievement pressures of accountability, by the enrollment threats of school choice, and by the fiscal demands of the recession. Yet the districts remain weak. Where districts have been willing to fight for effective organization, it has almost always occurred (and then, only sometimes) in cities—most notably Washington, DC, New Haven, New York—where mayors have taken control of the schools. Even then, only partial progress has been made, and it is inherently vulnerable. Bold, reformist mayors ultimately leave office, as do their school chancellors, and their successors are unlikely to show the same resolve. Indeed, they may prove to be union allies.[6]

There are a few other districts where unusual changes are underway as well—for example, in Hillsborough County (FL), Memphis, and Pittsburgh, where heaps of money from the Gates Foundation have induced the unions to "collaborate" in teacher-evaluation reforms.[7] But in all these places, money has been the prime inducement for union collaboration, and their job interests remain a constant threat to progress going forward. How much change is actually achieved—how many teachers are actually dismissed due to poor performance, for example—remains to be seen.

The Politics of Blocking

For well over a quarter century, the NEA and the AFT have been the most powerful groups in the politics of education—with more than four million members, formidable sums of money for campaign contributions and lobbying, well-educated activists manning the electoral trenches, and organizations that blanket the nation, allowing them to coordinate all these resources toward political ends.[8]

Superior power doesn't mean that the teachers unions always get the policies they want. The American system of checks and balances makes that impossible, because its multiple veto points ensure that shepherding new laws through the political process is extremely difficult. The flip side, however, is that *blocking* new laws is much easier, for opponents need succeed at just *one* veto point to win. And this is how the teachers unions have used their political power in shaping the nation's schools: not by imposing the policies they want, but by blocking or weakening those they don't want—and thus preventing true reform. Throughout, they have relied on their alliance with the Democratic Party to do that. The teachers unions have been the raw power behind the politics of blocking. The Democrats have done the blocking.

The modern era's two great education reform movements, for school accountability and for school choice, attempt to bring major changes to the traditional structure of the American education system. Accountability seeks to put the spotlight on teacher performance, provide rigorous evaluations, link pay to performance, and move poor performers out of the classroom—all of which, from the unions' standpoint, are threatening departures from a traditional system in which performance was never seriously evaluated and all jobs were secure. School choice is highly threatening to the unions too. For when families are allowed to leave the regular public schools for new options—charter schools or (via vouchers or tax credits) private schools—the regular public schools lose money and jobs, and so do the incumbent teachers in those schools. And the unions lose members.

In recent years, choice advocates cheered because Indiana and Louisiana adopted new voucher programs and because charter schools—boosted by President Obama's Race to the Top program and movies like *Waiting for Superman*—continued to expand and attract supporters. But the bigger picture doesn't offer much to cheer about. The choice movement has been pushing for vouchers and tax credits since the 1980s, and as of 2013 these reforms still allow only about 200,000 children to attend private schools with government assistance. Compare this to a public school population of more than 50 million children. And charter schools? The first charter schools were authorized in Minnesota in 1991, and more than twenty years later, despite all the excitement surrounding them, charters enroll less than 5 percent of the nation's public school children. In most states and districts, they provide very little choice for American families and very little competition for the regular public schools. The explanation for the meager progress of school choice is very simple: the teachers unions (backed by school districts) have used their considerable power to stifle it.[9]

The same is true for accountability. Proponents are currently excited because, in the wake of Race to the Top, most states have passed laws requiring that teachers be evaluated with some reference to their performance. But again, what is the big picture? The big picture is that, throughout the entire reform era, teachers have not been seriously evaluated at all. Literally 99 percent of them have regularly received satisfactory evaluations. And almost never have teachers actually been dismissed merely for being incompetent. Why did the nation have to wait a quarter century to get even a modicum of change? The answer, again, is that the teachers unions are opposed to performance-based evaluations (as are most districts), and they have used their power over the years to stand in the way of genuine reform.

For accountability advocates, performance-based evaluation is their mountaintop of success. The rest of the educational landscape is littered with disappointments. The No Child Left Behind (NCLB) Act was a monumental achievement in 2001—and the union's greatest political defeat in the modern era—but in subsequent years it was NCLB that found itself being transformed, and ultimately eviscerated, by powerful political blowback from unions and the intransigence of the districts. Meantime, state accountability systems regularly test students—but do not, in fact, hold teachers or schools accountable for how much students learn and rarely impose any consequences for poor performance. No one loses a job. Real pay for performance remains a rarity. And the evidence so far is that, even in states that have passed new laws requiring rigorous, performance-based evaluation, virtually all teachers are getting satisfactory evaluations, just as before.[10]

The accountability movement has surely had an impact. The nation's focus is on performance now more than at any other time in the history of the public school system. Performance measures are made public. There is heightened pressure on school districts and teachers to raise test scores and promote learning. But the reality is that the nation's fifty-plus-one accountability systems do not actually hold anyone accountable. They are pale reflections of what well-designed accountability systems would actually do. They are the victims of power.

The Future

As long as the teachers unions remain powerful, America's schools cannot be organized in the best interests of children. At the local level, the unions use their power in collective bargaining to impose special-interest work rules that make no sense from the standpoint of effective schooling. In the policymaking process, they use their power to block or weaken reformist attempts to correct for the system's pathologies and produce top-flight performance.

Is there any hope that the problem of union power can somehow be overcome? Under normal conditions, the answer would be no. Yet these are *not* normal times. American education stands at a critical juncture—and due to an unusual confluence of events, the stars are lining up in a unique configuration that augurs well for major change.[11]

Endogenous Change

Two separate dynamics are at work. The first is arising endogenously *within* the education system and its politics. Reformers are gaining political strength, and the teachers unions are on the defensive as never before.

One reason is that the modern political environment has become increasingly polarized, and conservative Republicans—propelled by Tea Party devotees, the fiscal crisis, and big gains in the 2010 election—have taken on the unions like never before. In several states—Wisconsin, Indiana, Tennessee—they passed historically unprecedented legislation that limited collective bargaining and union prerogatives.[12] This is not, however, a uniform national phenomenon. And even in these few states, control of government will eventually shift to politicians more sympathetic to labor who will attempt to reverse course.

Another political development is more fundamental—and more damaging, in the long term, to the teachers unions. This one is taking place within the Democratic Party, where the unions' opposition to reform has led to increasing dissatisfaction—led by groups like Democrats for Education Reform, vocally expressed by moderate and liberal opinion leaders, energized by a growing network of education activists (many with roots in Teach for America), and funded by well-heeled philanthropists like Bill Gates and Eli Broad.[13] This ferment hasn't come close to converting most mainstream Democratic officeholders, who remain union allies. But President Barack Obama and his secretary of education, Arne Duncan, are clearly in the reform wing of the party, and they bucked the unions in 2009–10 with their Race to the Top, a competition for funds that induced states to pursue system-bending reforms. Since then, as I've noted, one of these reforms—performance-based evaluations—has become the centerpiece of the nation's reform agenda.[14]

The tide has turned against the teachers unions, and they are in defense mode. Yet even reformist Democrats, from Obama on down, have made it clear that they have no intention of taking action to limit collective bargaining or weaken the power of the unions. They are serious about improving the nation's schools. But they intend to do it collaboratively within an education system filled with powerful unions that must be accommodated and made "part of the solution." This intention is reinforced by a brute political fact: the power of the Democratic Party itself is highly dependent on the power of the unions, and thus on the continuation of collective bargaining.[15]

The political dynamic we are now witnessing in American education, then—an endogenous development that has emerged within the system itself—is not equipped to bring about major change. It propels the education system in the right direction. But it is inherently limited, because it does little to reduce the *power* of the teachers unions—and they will continue to use their power to prevent the schools from being effectively organized.

Something more is needed. Something that *does* reduce union power.

Exogenous Change

That something is the worldwide revolution in information technology—an exogenous development, originating entirely *outside* the education system, that is among the most profoundly influential forces ever to sweep the planet. With its roots in information and knowledge, it cannot help but transform the way students learn, teachers teach, and schools are organized. It is the future of American education—indeed, of world education.

Already, online curricula can be customized to the learning styles and life situations of individual students, giving them instant feedback on how well they are doing, providing them with remedial work when they need it, allowing them to move at their own pace, and giving them access—wherever they live, whatever their race or background—to a vast range of courses their own schools don't offer and, ultimately, to the best the world can provide. By strategically substituting technology (which is cheap) for labor (which is expensive), moreover, schools can be far more cost-effective than they are now—which is crucial in a future of tight budgets.[16]

Because technology stands to have enormous impacts on jobs and money, the teachers unions find it threatening. And throughout the 2000s, they have used their political power—in state legislatures, in the courts—to try to slow and stifle its advance. But they won't succeed forever. Education technology is a tsunami that is only now beginning to swell, and it will hit the American public school system with full force over the next decade and those to follow. Long term, the teachers unions can't stop it. It is much bigger and more powerful than they are.

The advance of technology will then have dire consequences for established power. There will be a growing substitution of technology for labor and thus a steep decline in the number of teachers (and union members) per student; a dispersion of the teaching labor force, which will no longer be so geographically concentrated

in districts (because online teachers can be anywhere); and a proliferation of new online providers and choice options, attracting away
students, money, and jobs. All of these developments will dramatically undermine the membership and financial resources of the
teachers unions, and thus their political power. Increasingly, they
will be *unable to block*, and the political gates will swing open—to
yield a new era in American education.[17]

Hastening the Future

Whether this future arrives quickly or takes many decades will
depend in part on what researchers can do to shed light on the
problem of union power—and, more generally, on the key roles
that the teachers unions play in American education, its politics,
and its reform. This is the kind of information policymakers need
if they are to pursue reforms that stand to be truly effective.

To date, shockingly little research has been carried out on teachers unions. Here are some of the key areas that call out for serious
study.

- What is the impact of collective bargaining on the costs of public education, the organization of the schools, and the academic
  achievement of students?[18]

- What role do teachers unions play in school board elections,
  how successful are they in selecting sympathetic district leaders,
  and how does this electoral connection affect the unions' influence in district policymaking and collective bargaining?

- How do the unions use their power in the "politics of blocking" to try to stifle education reform, particularly at the state
  level (where authority over the schools mainly resides), how successful are they—and what factors explain their lack of success
  when reforms actually get adopted?

- In the Southern and border states, teachers unions often don't
  have collective bargaining rights—but they are still organized,
  have members and money, and are quite active politically.

How does their exercise of power in these contexts—at both the state and local levels—compare to what happens in the alleged "strong union" states? Are the unions really weaker in the Southern and border states than they are elsewhere, and are the differences significant?

- On performance-based evaluations and other post-Race to the Top reforms, how does "collaboration" with the teachers unions—in filling out the details, in the implementation process—affect the reforms' ultimate content and impact? Does "collaboration" lead to weaker, less effective reforms?

- Does the recent reformist ferment within their party lead Democrats to embrace bold reforms of real consequence? Or does it lead them to embrace only those reforms that are "collaboratively" determined and compatible with continuing union power?

- How have the unions dealt with the rise of educational technology—how have they tried to control it, how have they tried to defeat it, in what ways have they "supported" it?

- How is the advance of technology affecting the unions' ability to organize and wield influence, to what extent is it attracting new players into K–12 education—and, overall, how is it affecting the balance of power in the politics of reform?

These topics only scratch the surface. For too long, education researchers have virtually ignored the teachers unions, focusing their attention on curricula, teaching methods, testing, and other components of the process of schooling—all of which are important—but bypassing the larger considerations of power and special interest that profoundly shape the system as a whole, including its individual schools and what happens within them. If policymakers are to understand the American school system and, in particular, if they are to understand it well enough to devise truly effective reforms, this needs to change.

Notes

1. National Commission on Excellence in Education, *A Nation at Risk: The Imperative for Educational Reform* (Washington, DC: US Department of Education, 1983); Thomas Toch, *In the Name of Excellence: The Struggle to Reform the Nation's Schools, Why It's Failing, and What Should Be Done* (New York: Oxford University Press, 1991); and Eric A. Hanushek and Alfred A. Lindseth, *Schoolhouses, Courthouses, and Statehouses: Solving the Funding-Achievement Puzzle in America's Public Schools* (Princeton, NJ: Princeton University Press, 2009).

2. Terry M. Moe, *Special Interest: Teachers Unions and America's Public Schools* (Washington, DC: Brookings Institution Press, 2011).

3. For documentation on members' ties to their unions, as well as on issues of collective bargaining, see Moe, *Special Interest*, chaps. 3–5.

4. For analyses of the impact of collective bargaining on student outcomes, see Caroline M. Hoxby, "How Teachers' Unions Affect Education Production," *Quarterly Journal of Economics* 111, no.3 (1996): 671–718; see also Terry M. Moe, "Collective Bargaining and the Performance of the Public Schools," *American Journal of Political Science* 53 (2009): 156–174; and for an overview of the literature, see Moe, *Special Interest*, chap. 5.

5. Terry M. Moe, "Teachers Unions and School Board Elections," in *Besieged: School Boards and the Future of Education Politics*, ed. William G. Howell (Washington, DC: Brookings Institution Press, 2005); and Terry M. Moe, "Political Control and the Power of the Agent," *Journal of Law, Economics, & Organization* 22 (2006): 1–29.

6. Moe, *Special Interest*; Joseph Viteritti, ed., *When Mayors Take Charge: School Governance in the City* (Washington, DC: Brookings Institution Press, 2008);

Jeffrey R. Henig and Wilbur C. Rich, eds., *Mayors in the Middle: Politics, Race, and Mayoral Control of Urban Schools* (Princeton, NJ: Princeton University Press, 2003); and Kenneth K. Wong, Francis X. Shen, Dorothea Anagnostopoulos, and Stacey Rutledge, *The Education Mayor: Improving America's Schools* (Washington, DC: Georgetown University Press, 2007).

7. United Press International, "Gates Foundation Program Aimed at Schools," November 18, 2009, www.upi.com /Top_News/US/2009/11/18/Gates-Foundation-program -aimed-at-schools/UPI-46821258569176; Nick Anderson, "Gates Foundation Playing Pivotal Role in Changes for Education System," *Washington Post,* July 12, 2010.

8. For evidence on the arguments in this section, see Moe, *Special Interest,* chaps. 9 and 10.

9. For a summary of the evidence on choice, see Moe, *Special Interest,* chaps. 9 and 10.

10. On this last point, see Jenny Anderson, "Curious Grade for Teachers: Nearly All Pass," *New York Times,* March 30, 2013. For a summary of the evidence on accountability, see Moe, *Special Interest,* chaps. 9 and 10.

11. On critical junctures and how they figure into analyses of institutional change, see Paul Pierson, *Politics in Time: History, Institutions, and Social Analysis* (Princeton, NJ: Princeton University Press, 2004).

12. See, e.g., Richard Locker, "Tennessee Legislature OK's Ban of Teacher Bargaining," *Commercial Appeal* (Memphis, TN), May 20, 2011.

13. See, e.g., Steven Brill, *Class Warfare: Inside the Fight to Fix America's Schools* (New York: Simon and Schuster, 2011).

14. On Race to the Top, see Moe, *Special Interest,* and Brill, *Class Warfare.* On state laws requiring performance-based evaluations, see National Council on Teacher Quality, "State of the States 2012: Teacher Effectiveness Policies" (Washington, DC: National Council on Teacher Quality, 2012).

15. For a detailed discussion of the prospects for "reform unionism," see Moe, *Special Interest*, chaps. 8 and 10.

16. Clayton M. Christensen, Michael B. Horn, and Curtis W. Johnson, *Disrupting Class: How Disruptive Innovation Will Change the Way the World Learns* (New York: McGraw-Hill, 2008); Terry M. Moe and John E. Chubb, *Liberating Learning: Technology, Politics, and the Future of American Education* (San Francisco: Jossey-Bass, 2009); and Paul E. Peterson, *Saving Schools: From Horace Mann to Virtual Learning* (Cambridge, MA: The Belknap Press of Harvard University Press, 2010).

17. Moe and Chubb, *Liberating Learning*.

18. This is the one area in which there is an empirical literature. Much of it is dated or of poor quality, however, and a great deal more needs to be done if the questions here are to be answered with confidence. For an overview of this literature, see Moe, *Special Interest*, chap. 6.

Part II: *Crucial Changes*

CHAPTER 4

Transforming via Technology

John E. Chubb

Forty-eight students in a class. That may sound like a post-recessionary public school nightmare. But it is not. It is the design of a new public charter school that "blends" teachers and technology. Class sizes are large because students spend only part of their class time receiving instruction from the teacher. Broken into smaller groups, students rotate during class from the teacher to technology to other activities. The teacher is never trying to instruct forty-eight students directly; group sizes for instruction are small. In this blended model the teacher is both instructor of students and facilitator of students learning themselves.

For at least a generation—since the takeoff of the Internet, if not longer—educators have asked how technology will help students learn. Outside of school, the Internet and ever more accessible devices enable students, and adults, to access information, conduct research, and receive instruction about an infinite variety

This work was supported in part by a generous grant from the Walton Family Foundation to Education Sector. The views expressed are those of the author and should not be ascribed to the Foundation.

of topics with increasing ease. But schools struggle to incorporate online resources and computers into the education process. The tired observation that schools and classrooms look much the same today as fifty or a hundred years ago is nonetheless true. As obvious as it may be that the technologies that inform us outside of school should enhance learning inside school, this has simply not come to pass.

But finally it may be. The Alliance Tennenbaum Family Technology High School, with forty-eight students in a class, is just one example of models nationally that are rapidly providing students with substantial access to technology.[1] In the process, they are opening up new ways for students to learn. This is obviously important. American students need to acquire new skills to participate in the technologically sophisticated world in which they already live. They also need to master traditional knowledge and skills as successfully as students worldwide—something US students are not doing well at present.[2] The Alliance High School offers new opportunities to students who need them most. Located in East Los Angeles and serving predominately poor Latino students with a history of dropping out, the school is demonstrating that "blended learning" can actually change lives.

From schools like Alliance that mix technology and teachers in every classroom, to schools that allow students to choose to take courses either traditionally or online, to schools that serve students full-time online, technology is finally changing the ways that students receive instruction. To be sure, most US students are still taught the old-fashioned way. But the future is beginning rapidly to unfold. One need look no further than higher education to see the possibilities clearly. Students routinely learning online, universities scrambling and competing for a role in this dynamic new world, elite universities offering massive open online courses (MOOCs) for free—the media bring us daily developments. K–12 education moves more slowly, but just as the changes in higher education are today unmistakable, soon they will be obvious in America's schools.

The Driving Force

Schools are inherently conservative institutions. Responsible for the welfare of children, they appropriately approach experimentation and innovation with caution. All types of schools—private, public, public charter—show similar respect for the tried-and-true: students grouped in age-graded classrooms taught and supervised by a teacher. Traditional public schools are also slowed by the political process that governs them. Status quo interests, represented by teachers' unions and other well-heeled organizations, wield disproportionate influence in elections and the legislative process. They can often block or weaken reforms that threaten resources and roles in existing schools.[3] It has been thirty years since a landmark federal education report declared us *A Nation at Risk*. Every major school reform since—charter schools, higher academic standards, testing and accountability—has faced stiff resistance from the public school establishment and proceeded only after serious compromise.

It is easy to assume that much the same fate awaits today's technologies. Computers have actually been in schools since the time of *A Nation at Risk*. Every public school has been connected to the Internet for over a decade.[4] Schools have taken every other technological innovation in stride, beginning with television—predicted to be a game-changer in its day. Technology *is* a threat to jobs in the current system. If students can learn on their own over the Internet, they will require fewer teachers, at least of the familiar classroom variety. Teachers' unions have consequently fought state authorization of online charter schools, which take students and funding away from traditional schools much as brick-and-mortar charter schools have been doing since they were first authorized over twenty years ago. Technological innovation *has* been slow. Schools by and large teach much as they always have. Technology appears to be having about the same effect as every other serious school reform.

But technology is different. Technology is not an education reform, dependent on the education system for its development. Technological innovation—specifically the development of Internet-based electronic data, resources, computing, and communication—is a worldwide sector-spanning phenomenon. Fueled by industries and a society more open to innovation than education, and with more incentives to adopt and adapt, information technology is evolving rapidly and inexorably. Technology has fundamentally altered how every business does its work, generally enhancing productivity in the process. Companies like Google, Apple, and Amazon have transformed how we access information and media. Students and their parents—not to mention educators themselves—now learn regularly through online interactions, as accessible as a mobile application. Essential teaching and learning technologies emerge and evolve every day—industry needs them, society needs them—whether K–12 education participates or not. No law needs to be passed; no political opposition needs to be overcome.

It is only a matter of time until information technologies fully penetrate and then fundamentally change K–12 schools. Conservative and resistant though they may be, schools are ultimately accountable to a public that pays taxes or tuition and expects its young people to achieve. Public schools in the United States already spend as much per pupil as any nation in the world. Private schools charge tuitions that have risen more rapidly than inflation for two generations. Much as higher education has run into severe criticism for its high costs, K–12 education is finding it nigh impossible to ask parents or the public for more dollars. The recession of 2008 and its long aftermath only tightened public finances further. K–12 schools *need* technology to curtail expenses: with 60 percent of all expenditures in K–12 schools going to instructional salaries and 85 percent to personnel overall, schools cannot become materially more efficient without labor-saving technology. Today's innovations hold that promise, especially those that enable students to learn more independently.[5]

And, learning really is the key. Schools are already looking for efficiencies, to limit budget cuts in the public school sector and to retain tuition-strapped parents in the private. But technology would not be nearly as attractive if it merely helped schools accomplish the same for less. Technology is compelling because it has the potential to help more students learn more successfully. Technology can enhance the learning experience for students and increase the effectiveness and reach of teachers.

Students working online have the chance to move through lessons at their own pace, not at a classroom pace inevitably too slow for some and too fast for others. Students can be taught online through print, voice, video, animation, and simulation—multimedia not so easily available in a classroom. Students can work interactively online, responding to regular prompts and challenges built into the instructional software. Students can be assessed as often as necessary to ensure they are on track. They can be tutored, electronically or by a teacher online, with custom lessons matched to weaknesses exposed by ongoing assessments. They can conduct research and experiments and produce multimedia products and presentations. Students can collaborate through social media, much as they would be expected to collaborate some day at work. Indeed, it is hard to imagine students learning twenty-first century skills, which experts generally believe should supplement traditional academics, without new technology-infused approaches to learning.

Teachers can benefit from online instruction as well. If they are teaching online, they may find that they can provide more personalized instruction because electronic media are doing the heavy lifting of core instruction. If they are teaching in a mixed or blended classroom, they should find more opportunity to instruct higher-order skills and promote research and projects. The computer can present the basic knowledge and skills. The teacher can help students apply them. Classrooms can be "flipped," students experiencing lectures at home online and interacting with teachers on assignments at school. Whether teaching online or in a blended brick-and-mortar environment, teachers will find much better access to student performance data. Teachers will have comprehensive "grade books" that integrate data from multiple online and traditional assessments and programs, helping teachers stay on top of student progress. Teachers will be provided with differentiated assignments for students who need remediation or acceleration. And they will be offered online professional development to support any new instructional skills or content they may need.[6]

Technology offers all of these features today in some fashion. And technology is steadily improving as rising usage spurs investment in its development. Unlike our schools, which improve only slowly as they try to coax gains from an age-old model, technology should continue to improve substantially. It is a relatively new model of education—and one that is already working. A meta-analysis sponsored by the US Department of Education found that students working online achieve at least as much as students learning in traditional classrooms.[7] A recent large-scale randomized trial found that students in beginning statistics courses learned as much working fully online as students taking traditional classes—but at a fraction of the price.[8] Models blending online and classroom instruction are showing promising results, striving to get the best from both technology and teachers. Problems remain, to be sure. Student retention can be an issue if online instruction is not well-supported by teachers or if students are not ready for the independence.[9] But the evidence is growing that online education is helping more students succeed.

With its success, technology is being adopted. More than half of all school districts report using online instruction in some way.[10] Most of this usage, to be clear, is for coursework outside of the core academic program. Students are mostly working online when their schools cannot practically or economically offer courses in traditional classrooms. Advanced Placement classes with too little demand to fill a section, "credit recovery" classes for students who failed a class the first time, or off-hour classes for students who have dropped out of high school—these are among the most common uses of online instruction. The district saves money moving students online and regular teaching positions are not threatened. School districts also make extensive use of remedial reading and math programs, to help elementary and middle school students catch up to their classmates. These uses are hardly the stuff of revolutionary change. But they are also just the beginning.

Competition and Choice

School districts cannot be expected to engage in revolution. Left to their own devices, they would incorporate technology incrementally, slowly—safely. That is what online AP, credit recovery, and the like are all about. Technology has not left it at that. Over the last decade, the advance of technology, outside and inside of education, has inspired policymakers in a few places to push aside opposition and offer students new ways to access technology-based education. Most of the action has been at the state level, though some districts have had the will as well.

Legislation authorizes institutions other than traditional public schools to provide public education online. Legislation concomitantly provides students and their families the right to choose education online, with and without approval from traditional public schools. They can choose online education both full-time and part-time.[11]

Twenty years ago state legislators began to approve charter schools in order to give families public school options other than their district or neighborhood schools. Today, forty-one states and the District of Columbia permit charter schools. Nearly 6,000 charter schools enroll over two million students, approaching 4 percent of all public school students.[12] This is remarkable growth, and a generally positive influence on public education—for the students choosing charter schools and the traditional schools spurred to compete with them.[13] The results have not been consistently good. But charter schools have won bipartisan support for being a largely positive force for change, especially for disadvantaged students who are most in need of better schools.[14]

Legislators have chosen similar measures to spur technological innovation.[15] States that permit brick-and-mortar charter schools are increasingly authorizing charter schools that serve full-time students completely or mostly online. These schools often serve entire states or at least multiple school districts. Students from rich and poor neighborhoods have access to the same online schools, an opportunity that brick-and-mortar charter schools cannot duplicate. Home-schooled students, who number 1.8 million nationally, have access to instruction otherwise unavailable to them. Legislators have also authorized state-operated virtual schools. These new entities offer students the opportunity to take individual courses online as well as, occasionally, to enroll full-time. For individual courses, legislation usually gives students the right to choose most any course, with limited guidance or veto power by their school of record.

A few states—Florida, Pennsylvania, and Utah being exemplars—are on their way to creating a dynamic of choice and competition in cyberspace. Students have more full-time and part-time options than choice in the brick-and-mortar world could ever create. As states become more accommodating, providers of online instruction have entrepreneurial outlets for their content; they need not depend on reluctant school districts as their only customers. Because the dynamic is at the course level as well as the school level, it has the potential to be far more disruptive to the status quo than traditional school choice. Whereas relatively few students may use school choice to improve their educational prospects, many if not most students may use course choice. The early numbers bear out expectations. Over two million students are already choosing online learning as a public education alternative.[16]

Response and Counter-Response

The growth of online education, in all of its forms, has been driven by the inexorable development of information technology itself and by the competitive dynamic that state policymakers are beginning to create by extending choice to cyberspace. Online providers are responding to the new demand with a proliferation of offerings. Traditional public schools have countered with their own offerings. Competition has enriched the options for students and accelerated the use of information technology in schools of all kinds.

As of 2012, cyber-charter schools operated in thirty-one states, or three-fourths of the states that allow brick-and-mortar charter schools.[17] Where cyber-charters have not yet emerged, they are either proscribed by the charter school law or funded too poorly to be viable. These new online schools enroll about 275,000 students nationwide. In states with firmly established schools, the growth in enrollments has been strong: about 15 percent per year. State laws have a major influence on enrollments, and growth rates have varied accordingly by state. Five states—Arizona, Ohio, Pennsylvania, California, and Colorado—enroll about half of the nation's full-time online charter school students. If all states that authorize charter schools had laws similar to these five, enrollments overall would no doubt be much larger. Some charter laws limit enrollment geographically or numerically; other laws, like New York's and New Jersey's, prohibit cyber-charters. Demand for full-time online schools is likely well above the 275,000 students enrolled today.[18]

Still, most students interested in online education will not want to skip the traditional school experience altogether. They will want social learning experiences, proximity to friends, and the panoply of extracurricular activities available in many brick-and-mortar schools. While online schools find ways to assemble students for activities of various kinds—including an annual prom—online schools largely have students working at home, supervised by a parent. This is not every parent's cup of tea either, especially working parents.

Policymakers have offered students a part-time option, most often provided by a state-sponsored virtual school.[19] In 2012, twenty-seven states had such schools with total enrollment of 619,847. The most recent annual growth rate was 16 percent. As with full-time cyber-charters, student participation varies widely across the nation as a result of state policies. One state, Florida, saw over 300,000 course enrollments, nearly half of the national total. The Florida Virtual School is one of the oldest state cyberschools. But its size is not a product of its age. Florida policymakers gave students the right to choose most any course in the state secondary school curriculum and receive school credit, without school permission—and used the student's pro-rated local per-pupil funding to pay the state. The program was thereby self-financing, and generously so. States with fewer enrollments may require a student's home school to give permission—which it may resist if that would jeopardize sufficient enrollment in core school offerings. Less successful states may fund their state virtual schools with extra appropriations, rather than regular public school aid, thereby limiting course offerings. Nevertheless, six states have state-sponsored virtual schools enrolling over 15,000 students per year. One of them, North Carolina, is approaching 100,000 course enrollments annually.

In all, state law enabled 900,000 students nationwide to participate in online education outside of their local school districts, full-time or part-time. That is less than 2 percent of all public school students. But a higher percentage of high school students participated. They constitute most of the course-takers and a large portion of the full-time students. Traditional public schools have taken notice and are fighting back.

In Pennsylvania, school districts have banded together to create their own full- and part-time online schools. Pennsylvania is one of the largest cyber-charter markets in the country, with over 32,000 full-time enrollments in 2012 and continued double-digit growth. Districts pay cyber-charters about $9,000 per pupil. In recent years, Intermediate Education Units (IUs)—multi-district consortia that provide various services to member school districts—have created online schools. Individual school districts often lack the scale to open their own online schools, so their IUs have taken up the challenge.[20] Chester County, outside of Philadelphia, offered online education to students in thirty-eight school districts; Philadelphia recently became the thirty-ninth. Philadelphia currently pays to send 6,000 students to online charter schools each year. It hopes to shift 1,000 students to the Chester County–run school, saving $4,000 per student. Similar IU-run schools surround Pittsburgh and Harrisburg, the latter enrolling 1,200 full-time students after just four years of operation. Exact counts of multi-district schools are not available for every state, but most states have IU's—or districts big enough to create their own online schools. Cyber-charters and state virtual schools should expect continued competition from school districts.

The most exciting competition is from blended schools, like the Alliance High School with which we began. No one believes that the best education model for students is completely online, regardless of who the provider might be. Students can learn a great deal working online and interacting with electronic media. They also have much to learn from teachers, their peers, and face-to-face interaction. Students really need both forms of instruction. The challenge is finding the right mixes for different students and subjects. Schools are now experimenting, and at a quickening pace.

The most radical experiments are in charter schools, where rules governing class size, teacher assignments, and seat time (awarding credit for hours in class rather than mastery of subject matter) do not strictly apply.[21] Rocketship Education, based in San Jose, California, runs seven schools and is expanding to Milwaukee in 2013. It aims eventually to work in fifty cities and serve one million students. Carpe Diem began in Arizona and expanded in 2012 to Indiana. It too has ambitious growth objectives. Other emerging models include Nexus Academy, run by Connections, a division of Pearson Education and operator of numerous cyber-charters, and Touchstone Education, based in Newark, New Jersey. Like Alliance, these charter models radically change the school day to personalize education for every student, aiming to provide each the optimal combination of teacher-directed experiences and online education.

These schools are working with students in different physical spaces, not traditional classrooms. Teachers are playing a range of roles with their students, not leading whole group instruction. School financial arrangements are also different, with fewer teachers and more technology than traditional schools. The hope is that net savings can be used to raise the compensation of individual teachers. Blended schools could potentially attract and retain top talent by paying teachers more for serving more students—in "high tech, high touch" fashion.[22]

Traditional public schools do not have the flexibility to be as inventive with their blends. But creative models are emerging. Nashville, Tennessee, and Charlotte-Mecklenburg, North Carolina, school districts are using blended models to extend the reach of their most successful teachers.[23] The Chicago public schools operate several different blended models, including VOISE (Virtual Opportunities Inside a School Environment) Academy, part of the district's ambitious Renaissance 2010 new schools program. Firm counts of blended public schools—traditional or charter—do not exist. The Innosight Institute, which tracks and supports blended learning, has identified scores of organizations and companies that work with schools to implement blended models.[24]

Research Could Help Make the Difference

Online learning is already being used in the majority of the nation's school districts. Outside of the districts, in cyber-charter schools, blended charter schools, state virtual schools, and multi-district online schools, public education is offering students something quite different. Well over two million public school students now participate annually in online learning in traditional and non-traditional venues. That's more than double the figure just five years ago. Students and families—and a new generation of teachers raised in the digital world themselves—will demand better use of information technology in public education. Yes, there is resistance. But policymakers have provided just enough choice for families and openings for competitors to serve the rising demand. The great breakthrough in recent years is the development of educational models that aim to bring students the best of what both teachers and technology have to offer. Schools really are becoming different this time.

In the grand scheme of things the precise direction and pace of these changes will be determined more by the forces of politics, the economy, and technology itself. But, public policy will also play an important role, and that work could and should be shaped by research. What is not known about education and technology is vast. Advocates and opponents fuel the debate with self-serving "analysis." Now is the time for serious research to provide policymakers with more factual guidance. Several issues are ripe for analysis.

For all of the encouraging evidence of student progress online, we have little systematic evidence of what instructional models work best. Data on student achievement, demographics, and school attributes are strong for full-time online schools. They are public schools, after all, and must comply with testing and reporting requirements like brick-and-mortar schools. Research could already begin to clarify success factors for cyber-charters and other full-time online schools. But even with decent data, that task is not straightforward. Students who select full-time online learning may differ from traditional students in unmeasured ways, confounding comparison between innovation and the status quo. Many full-time online students enroll for only a year or two—intentionally—and then return to regular schools, making common statistics like graduation rates or one-time high school assessments imperfect measures of performance. These technical issues can certainly be addressed, but currently we have no strong studies of full-time online schooling.

Part-time online instruction has been studied even less—and here is where most future enrollments will surely lie. States generally do not keep track of individual student course-taking, even if the courses are taken at state-run schools. Districts do not keep systematic track either. We have no common assessments of student success at the course level. Estimates of the volume of course-taking nationally, cited above, are based on spottily reported data and guesstimates in other places with known course-taking activity. As a result of the data gaps, we do not know how much course-taking is by advanced students, remedial students, or regular students. This question is important, because it is the regular students whose participation indicates a real opening up of the traditional system. A national study just documenting course-taking would be a huge contribution to the state of knowledge.

Blended-learning models are another gaping hole. Anecdotes abound highlighting new learning spaces and new roles for teachers and technology, as already described. But we know little systematically about the varying attributes of models, their incidence, or their effects on learning. We also know nothing of the business models that might make blended-learning schools more efficient. Descriptive studies of significant samples of schools would be very useful, before sophisticated analyses are even contemplated. And on the point of business models, uncertainties extend well beyond blended models: the economics of online instruction, including MOOCs, have not been worked out in higher education, not to mention K–12. We have as much to learn about the business of online learning as we do about the educational proposition.

Finally, there is the matter of public policy. It is clear already that technology adoption varies by state. Terry Moe and I first reported on the variations in *Liberating Learning* in 2009: the stronger the organized opposition to technology, the more limited the adoptions. In ensuing years, many states have moved to adopt more open-access measures and online learning activity has increased, predictably unevenly, across the nation. But policymakers really do not know what laws are the most important levers of change. If research could document the use of online learning full- and part-time more accurately and completely, it could then help policymakers understand how to promote online learning most effectively.

The good news, however, should not be lost amid all of this uncertainty. Online and blended learning are increasing rapidly. Technology is pushing its way into education as policymakers provide just enough openings and technology itself proves its worth. This time *will* be different. But differences could come sooner, and with greater benefit for students, if research were a better guide.

Notes

1. The school is examined in Susan Headden, "The Right Mix: How One Los Angeles School is Blending a Curriculum for Personalized Learning," *Education Sector,* February 6, 2013.

2. For a recent analysis, see Eric A. Hanushek, Ludger Woessmann, and Paul E. Peterson, "Is the US Catching Up? International and State Trends in Student Achievement," *Education Next* 12, no. 4 (Fall 2012).

3. The resistance to education technology and its eventual breakdown are analyzed in Terry M. Moe and John E. Chubb, *Liberating Learning: Technology, Politics, and the Future of American Education* (San Francisco: Jossey-Bass, 2009).

4. For statistics over time on technology in schools, see "Technology Counts," *Education Week,* March 15, 2012, and earlier annual reports.

5. On education spending domestically and internationally, and its implications for teacher quality, see John E. Chubb, *The Best Teachers in the World: Why We Don't Have Them and How We Could* (Stanford, CA: Hoover Institution Press, 2012), chap. 2.

6. For a description of blended models, see Peter W. Cookson, "Blended Learning: Creating the Classroom of Tomorrow Today" (Alexandria, VA: ASCD, 2013).

7. Barbara Means, Yukie Toyama, Robert Murphy, Marianna Bakia, and Karla Jones, "Evaluation of Evidence-Based Practices in Online Learning: A Meta-Analysis and Review of Online Learning Studies" (Washington, DC: US Department of Education, 2010).

8. See Steve Kolowich, "Score One for the Robo-Tutors," *Inside Higher Ed*, May 22, 2012.

9. On the persistence problem and potential remedies, see Mandy Zatynski, "Calling for Success: Online Retention Rates Get Boost from Personal Outreach," *Education Sector,* January 16, 2013.

10. John Watson, Amy Murin, Lauren Vashaw, Butch Gemin, and Chris Rapp, *Keeping Pace with K–12 Online and Blended Learning: An Annual Review of Policy and Practice* (Durango, CO: Evergreen Education Group, 2012), 20–21.

11. The status of legislation authorizing, funding, and regulating online learning at the state level is detailed in "2012 Digital Learning Report Card," Digital Learning Now! an Initiative of the Foundation for Excellence in Education.

12. For current statistics, see Center for Education Reform, "National Charter School and Enrollment Statistics 2011–2012."

13. For a rigorous study of charter school performance, see Caroline M. Hoxby, Sonali Murarka, and Jenny Kang, "How New York City's Charter Schools Affect Student Achievement: August 2009 Report" (Cambridge, MA: New York City Charter Schools Evaluation Project, September 2009).

14. For the mixed results, see Center for Research on Education Outcomes, "Charter School Growth and Replication," Stanford University, January 2013.

15. On the challenges and opportunities for state online policy, see John E. Chubb, "Overcoming the Governance Challenge in K–12 Online Learning," in *Creating Sound Policy for Digital Learning* (Washington, DC: Thomas B. Fordham Institute, February 16, 2012).

16. Based on estimates of the gamut of student uses in Watson et al., *Keeping Pace*, 20–33.

17. Statistics in this section are from ibid., 24–27.

18. For more on the effects of state laws, see Chubb, "Overcoming the Governance Challenge."

19. See Watson, *Keeping Pace*, 29–32.

20. See Benjamin Herold, "Philadelphia to Launch Online School," NBC 10 Philadelphia, April 20, 2013.

21. On blended charter models see Chubb, *The Best Teachers in the World*, chap. 2; and Watson, *Keeping Pace*, 23–24.

22. For a national model of savings from technology and increased compensation for teachers, see Chubb, *The Best Teachers in the World*, chap. 2.

23. For models extending the reach of top teachers, see Public Impact, "Extending the Reach of Excellent Teachers," February 2013.

24. Heather Staker, "The Rise of K–12 Blended Learning: Profiles of Emerging Models" (Mountain View, CA: Innosight Institute, 2011).

CHAPTER 5

Expanding the Options

Herbert J. Walberg

After decades of struggle, school choice has turned corners in scope, legislation, and the results of effectiveness research. School choice means that families can choose what they believe is the best public or private (that is, independent or parochial) school for their children. As documented here, school choice resembles free enterprise in encouraging innovation, competition, reduced costs, better performance, and accommodation to a variety of parental preferences.

Still far from its full potential in the United States and much of the rest of the world, school choice offers not only hope but solid evidence that transformed choice-centered school systems can perform well at lower costs to the great benefit of children, families, and both developing and advanced economies.[1] Today's challenge to scholars and policymakers is to make better known the scope, variety, and effectiveness of school choice and to carry out rigorous research on the kinds and conditions of school choice that work best to improve learning that promotes economic progress in advanced and developing economies.

This chapter was presented for discussion at a World Bank and United Kingdom Department of International Education conference.

The traditional American public school system hasn't risen to new international achievement standards. In the most recent international achievement survey, US students ranked twenty-seventh in mathematics and twenty-first in science. National surveys indicate 70 percent of American eighth graders cannot read proficiently, and most never catch up. About 1.2 million students drop out of high school each year; 44 percent of dropouts younger than twenty-four are jobless.

Yet, except for Luxembourg, the United States recently had the highest per-student spending in the world among advanced economies. With poor performance and high spending, American public schools are grossly inefficient. They are also grossly unfair, because poor families are typically confined to the worst schools in big cities. Their children drop out at higher rates than do their age peers. Similarly, developing countries with limited material resources might benefit greatly from school choice that provides generally high achievement and also differentiated schools, including those for fast learners.

Long-Term Consequences

Though student learning is the most important short-term outcome, it also has long-term consequences. Former US Secretary of State George Shultz and fellow Koret Task Force member Eric Hanushek[2] estimate that if American school mathematics scores were comparable to Canada's over the next twenty years, the GNP would improve by $70 billion over the next eighty years, equivalent to an income boost of 20 percent for each American worker. Citizens' abilities and knowledge are deciding factors in a nation's wealth, scientific progress, and economic freedom. The world's wealthiest nations have sustained strong intellectual traditions that result in notable accomplishments in engineering, mathematics, technology, and basic and applied science.

Cross-national studies emphasize the importance of encouraging exemplary learners to achieve as much as they are able.[3] Societies that support top performers in their efforts to maximize their abilities appear most likely to benefit all their citizens. Analyses of academic test scores from ninety countries suggest that, despite wide differences in culture, countries scoring highest made the most economic progress. In particular, countries with large percentages of students in the top 5 percent of all countries' scores grew their economies fastest.[4]

If more students were to achieve at such levels, they and their nations would stand to benefit. To accommodate students with different levels of ability and specialized interests in mathematics, science, language, and other subjects, charter and private schools can offer more differentiated programs than traditional public schools that provide insufficient challenges.

Given such advantages and needs for school choice, why isn't it more widespread? Many obstacles have stood in the way and will likely continue unless schooling is substantially changed. As shown by Terry Moe,[5] for example, the teachers' unions have fiercely resisted charter schools and vouchers for private schools since their staffs need not belong to unions, resulting in diminished union membership and legislative influence. In addition, school boards have been particularly negligent since they are responsible for representing the interests of students, the community, and their nation. They have not held educators responsible for progress.

American teachers' unions have succeeded in instituting and maintaining tenure for poorly performing staff and the shortest school year—180 days—among advanced economies. Countries with the highest achievement have the longest school years—up to 260 days, plus after-school tutoring. Unionized school staff members, moreover, generally work about thirty hours per week for only nine months, in contrast to the typical American workweek of thirty-five to forty hours for a minimum of eleven months. Nominally responsible for children's achievement outcomes, public school boards seem uninformed, unconcerned, and unresponsive about poor teaching performance, excessive school costs, and students' meager achievement.

School Choice: Major Kinds, Growth, and Needed Research

The United States has expanded school choice in the last few decades, and much of the published world's research has been carried out in this country. Consider the growth and obstacles since 1990 to several forms of school choice:

- All but ten states now allow charter schools, which are supported with public funds but are privately governed and managed. With a Minnesota origin in 1991, charter schools in the United States now number nearly six thousand. Yet several states have no legislative provision for charter schools, and many states limit their number and size. Given the superior achievement of charter over traditional public schools (documented below), how can their numbers be expanded? What kinds, under what conditions, work best?

- Tuition tax credits are also growing in more than thirteen states. They allow parents to deduct private (that is, parochial and independent) school tuition and other education expenses from their state income taxes. (A special case is home-schooled students, estimated to be 1.5 million in 2007—a surprising 2.9 percent of all students—up from 850,000 in 1995. Home-schooled children typically excel their traditional public school peers.[6]) In March 2013, Alabama's governor signed sweeping legislation giving tax credits to parents who transfer their children from a failing public school to a private school of their choice. Yet most states severely limit the amount of tuition that can be deducted. How can such credits be expanded? What is the best amount of the credit? Should families that pay no taxes be subsidized?

- Traditional public educators adamantly resist vouchers, which are publicly or privately funded scholarships to families for their children to attend private schools. But vouchers appear on the possible verge of growth. In March 2013, the Indiana Supreme Court ruled that the state's 2011 Choice Scholarship Program is constitutional. The program allows poor families to receive vouchers equal to between 50 percent and 90 percent of the state per-pupil education funding to use in private schools. Yet few state legislatures seem likely to pass further voucher legislation unless members of the public, particularly parents, become better informed about positive voucher effects. Also, these groups would be better informed by rigorous research in their own states and they need to know what variations on voucher plans work best.

- As many as twenty states are considering "parent trigger" legislation, which closes failing schools upon a majority vote of parents and replaces the staff, charters the school for private management, or allows the students to attend private or other public schools. Yet only California has actually passed such legislation, and it only provides a weak alternative form that allows the failing staff to be dubiously "transformed" by additional training. Even though the parent trigger appears more acceptable than school closings to policymakers, since it is the parents who decide about the school which their children attend, why has so little numerical progress been made, and how can it be expanded? And can this form of school choice yield the superior results and lower costs that private and charter schools demonstrate?

Present Status of School Choice Research

A large 2007 corpus of research[7] in the United States and elsewhere shows that charter and private schools, which are referred to here as choice schools, excel in achievement, parent satisfaction, and students' social engagement. In the two most notably rigorous studies referenced in *School Choice: The Findings,* Caroline Hoxby and Paul Peterson, respectively, showed students "lotteried into" charter and private schools achieve more than students in nearby public schools who were "lotteried out." These studies are called randomized field trials and are increasingly recognized by social scientists as the most definitive in establishing causality, although observational studies that control for other probable causes can also be valuable.

An additional finding described in the book is that—though there are exceptions—the average cost of private schools in the United States is about half the cost of nearby public schools. This finding is particularly important in the United States since per-student public school costs are among the highest in the world. The finding is also important for developing countries with limited financial resources for schooling large populations of students.

Perhaps most impressive is the substantial appeal of charter and private schools. In big cities where poor residents and minorities are concentrated, as many as 80 percent of public school parents say they would send their children to private schools if they could afford the tuition. Tuition scholarships for poor families are heavily oversubscribed as are charter schools in areas where officials restrict the size and number of charter schools despite the many families that desire to enroll their children.

Recent research continues to show superior achievement performance of charter and private schools. In 2013, for example, The Mathematica Policy Research group published a multiyear study[8] of the Knowledge Is Power Program (KIPP), a network of charter schools with forty-one thousand students in twenty states. The study showed that after three years in the program, the students were eleven months ahead of their public school peers in math, eight months ahead in reading, and fourteen months ahead in science. Similarly, the Stanford University Center for Research on Education Outcomes[9] found in a 2013 study that after only a year, New York City charter school students gained substantially more in reading and math than their traditional school peers.

A Historical Pattern of School Choice

How could low achievement, high costs, and irresponsible supervision take place in American schools? In brief, the public school system over time became a huge set of ever-larger, poorly managed bureaucracies.[10] In colonial times, local citizens surrounding each small school could closely follow and supervise the school's budget and progress. Board members' children were often in the schools, which motivated them to inform themselves about the schools' staff and operations and to institute good policies.

In addition, public funds went to local private schools in the form of land grants and taxes from local residents. This was justified in that private schools provided a public service to the community. The fact that private schools were owned and managed by individuals, religious groups, or churches did not disqualify them from being considered "public" institutions when it came to funding, similar to the situation today in much of Asia and Europe. The United States is the outlier, which may be one of the reasons for its poor performance.

Local funding and control by small, well-informed groups of citizens were gradually eroded and finally lost. States consolidated roughly 115,000 small districts in 1900 into about 15,000 much larger districts today. Chicago, for example, has more than six hundred public schools. For this reason, today's public school boards are poorly informed about the many schools under their jurisdiction. Few big-city board members could name a fifth of the schools for which they are nominally responsible.

Since 1900, local control lost out in two other ways. States paid increasing shares of the total cost of schools and now pay on average about half of the costs. As schools' increasing expenditures consumed a large and growing share of state budgets, the states imposed complex rules and regulations on schools and in the last decade prescribed curriculum content and examinations.

Contributing around 10 percent of public school costs, the US Department of Education imposed further requirements and regulations on the public schools, which removed another major fraction of local boards' control over school policy. Both the federal and state departments of education have many specialized sub-departments that issue complex and sometimes conflicting rules with which local districts and schools must comply.

It might be said that when all these federal, state, and local departments and agencies are nominally responsible, none is truly responsible, and students, parents, and citizens are ill-served. Parents have little influence. Given a half-century of failure from school reform, great priority should be given to the further study of the effects of school choice in empowering parents over educators and school boards and its effects on advancing student achievement and parent satisfaction.

Size of Schools of Choice

From their one-room, one-teacher origins with as few as a dozen students, American schools grew ever more complex and larger, with as many as four thousand students in one Chicago school. Even though publicly funded, the schools in early American history were nearly "choice" schools, since tiny groups of parents and local residents could determine the mission, staffing, and operations in their local school. But many of today's parents, citizens, and legislators cannot inform themselves about the programs in ever-larger schools in ever-larger school districts. As schools grew larger, moreover, they became more departmentalized. A student in the middle grades may now have as many as five teachers, none of which know her well—one of the reasons big schools, other things being equal, tend to perform less well than others.[11]

One reason choice schools (private and charter) outperform their nearby traditional public schools is that they tend to be smaller. The parents, students, and staff are more likely to know each other. As a current example of ever-larger traditional public schools, the Chicago Board of Education is closing fifty traditional schools at one time and sending their students out of their neighborhoods to ever-larger schools against continuing parent protests.[12] As the late sociologist James S. Coleman pointed out,[13] large school size often leads to student alienation from the school and strong affiliation with what he called "the adolescent society." This society concentrates on things unconducive to learning such as cars, clothes, and dating in his day (perhaps television, computer games, and the Internet today) and distracts youths from adult influence, academic study, and constructive, active hobbies.

Avoiding Bureaucracy

Even with all these shortcomings, traditional public schools have endured as quasi-monopolies. Unless parents can afford tuition for private schools, gain their children's entrance to often oversubscribed charter schools, or move to neighborhoods with good schools, particularly in the suburbs, their children must go to the schools that the local district requires, usually on the basis of proximity to their homes. Choice schools (here meaning charter and private schools) in large cities, however, are less confined: to accommodate their interests, students can cross the school boundaries that confine traditional public school students. Small choice schools may also specialize in certain subjects and in beginning occupational and professional preparation in various fields. These specialties can attract families and students with common interests, in contrast to large traditional public schools that poorly serve students with disparate interests, aspirations, and levels of abilities.

Choice schools perform better and are more attractive to parents because they avoid the obstacles described above. They are usually small, and a well-informed board typically governs each school. Even national and regional boards of parochial schools usually govern with a light hand and leave many decisions and fundraising to local boards of single schools.[14]

Since they are free of most dysfunctional federal and state regulations, private and charter schools can readily develop programs that are appealing to the students and their families in the community. Should they fail to do so, they are likely to lose students. Continued failure may mean closure, leaving better schools to prosper.

Choice schools, moreover, need not hire teachers on the basis of governmental criteria used by public schools such as the number of education courses completed. They may heavily weigh advanced academic study and experience in the real world. Seldom unionized, moreover, choice schools pay teachers according to their contributions and performance. They may remove teachers who don't pull their weight.

Curriculum in Schools of Choice

Unlike traditional public schools, choice schools often restrict the curriculum largely to mathematics, science, English, a foreign language, history, political science, art, and music followed by all students, which best prepares them for college, careers, and citizenship. Avoiding the vast course miscellany and multiple specializations within large traditional public high schools, choice school students share a common academic and psychological experience. Unlike traditional public schools, moreover, choice schools are usually smaller and are rarely departmentalized. Thus, teachers know each other well and are informed about the content of subjects of classes other than their own. This enables them to avoid repetition while reinforcing central ideas across grades and subjects.

As mentioned above, however, in response to market demands, especially in big cities, some choice schools are known for concentrating on art, music, vocational studies, or other specializations that enable like-minded staff and students to intensively pursue their common interests, often with the cooperation of local museums, businesses, and other organizations. Students in such schools find motivation in these experiences. They also develop social bonds with one another and with their teachers and others that may help them in their careers.

Perhaps the least tangible advantage of choice schools is the act of choosing one. Even if a charter or private school were no better than a traditional forced-choice public school, the fact that parents and students themselves choose the school may mean they perceive distinct advantages in it, real or not. Wanting their choice to be a success, they may tend to make it so.

Private School Advantages

Private schools have several advantages over charter schools. States and municipalities may impose regulations on charter schools, which add to their costs and difficulties, that do not burden private schools.

Parochial schools have offered a means of continuing religiosity, community, and family stability for immigrant families as they become acculturated to American society. By choice, many of these and other private school families make financial sacrifices in order to maintain their family values and to avoid the drugs, gangs, delinquency, and teen pregnancy that plague some public schools, particularly in big cities. Such parents may believe that in an era of broken families, single parents, and divorce, parochial schools help maintain family cohesion.

In addition, the student compositions of the schools differ. Unless given scholarships or vouchers, families that send their children to private schools must readily afford or sacrifice to pay tuition. This of course means that their children will be with others from relatively affluent and motivated families that provide their children academically and socially constructive experiences before and during the school years—experiences less available to families whose children are confined to local public schools. Thus, private schoolchildren can benefit from student-peer groups better prepared by their families.

Multiplier Effects

As described in the introduction, a large body of studies in 2007[15] showed that, on average, choice school students excel in achievement. The research typically encompasses reading comprehension and mathematics but also sometimes includes the knowledge students gain in such subjects as English and science. As mentioned in the introduction, recent studies support this conclusion.

The studies showed, moreover, that the higher the percentage of students attending choice schools in a locality or state, the higher the average achievement of all schools. Studies of countries show the same pattern: the greater the percentage of students attending private schools, the higher the country's overall achievement. Private schools not only tend to excel but appear to raise the overall average even further by setting high standards and promoting competition among all schools.

Some of the comparative US studies reported on parents' satisfaction with their children's schools, the schools' reputations among nearby citizens, and the degree to which students were involved in the life of the school and engaged in volunteer work, such as tutoring other students and helping in community affairs. Again, private and charter schools excelled. Even so, more research is needed on how parents acquire knowledge of choice schools and how it may be increased.

School Choice Costs

As mentioned above, particularly important is the average annual per-student cost of schools since the United States typically ranks near the top among countries even though its achievement scores typically lag behind other industrialized countries. The US research on school choice costs, however, compares public and private schools (in this case not including charter schools). On average, educating students at private schools costs about half as much as it does at nearby public schools. Paul Peterson shows that competition among choice schools is an essential reason for their superior effectiveness and efficiency.[16]

These findings are consistent with research on an extensive variety of private organizations, including businesses. Other things being equal, they perform, on average, better than government-run organizations at lower costs, and they are more satisfying to their staff and their customers. Studies have examined airlines, banks, bus service, debt collection, electric utilities, forestry, hospitals, housing, insurance sales and processing, railroads, refuse collection, savings and loans, slaughterhouses, water utilities, and weather forecasting.

For this reason, governments in the United States and other countries, perhaps surprisingly, have begun to privatize prisons, police, fire protection, and public pensions.[17] Various experiments in privatization and "contracting out" of public services to competing for-profit and non-profit firms suggest they generally respond swiftly and accurately to contracted objectives and citizens' desires. If not, they forfeit continuation of their contracts, lose employees, decline in value, and often close. Better providers replace them.

Research Questions

In conclusion, given the consistency of positive results for school choice, unmet family preferences for it, cost savings, and the pressing need for better-educated students who will become tomorrow's workers and citizens, school choice should be greatly expanded. Progress in school choice has been made since 1990, but there is much further to go. Most feasible in the short term is wide promulgation of findings described in this chapter to families, taxpayers, and policymakers.

Much has been learned about school choice in the last two decades, but questions remain:

- Which forms of school choice work best—charter schools, vouchers, tuition tax credits, or parent triggers?

- Given the generally superior achievement, appeal, and cost-effectiveness of choice schools over traditional public schools, how can their numbers be expanded, and under what conditions do they work best?

- Since states severely limit the amount of tax tuition credits that can be deducted, how can such credits be expanded? What is the best amount of the credit? Should families that pay no taxes be subsidized for school and other education costs?

- Can the parent trigger yield the same generally superior results and lower costs as private and charter schools? Even though this approach appears more acceptable than vouchers since it is the parents who decide to close failing schools their children attend, why has so little legislative progress been made? How can legislation and participation be expanded?

- Finally, once school choice is widely in place, will parents be informed and empowered sufficiently well to remove their children from failing traditional *and* choice schools, and will such schools be closed? What organizations and methods would best provide legislators, citizens, and parents with good information on schools' achievement, features, parent satisfaction, and other important considerations? Can new private organizations (analogous to Consumers Union and J.D. Power and Associates) serve this purpose?

Notes

1. George P. Shultz and Eric Hanushek, "Education is the Key to a Healthy Economy," *Wall Street Journal*, May 1, 2012, http://hanushek.stanford.edu/publications/education-key

-healthy-economy; Eric Hanushek, "Interpreting Recent Research on Schooling in Developing Countries," *World Bank Research Observer* 10, no. 2 (August 1995): 227–246; and Eric Hanushek, "Economic Growth in Developing Countries: The Role of Human Capital," *Economics of Education Review* (forthcoming).

2. Shultz and Hanushek, "Education is the Key."

3. Herbert J. Walberg, "Scientific Literacy and Economic Productivity in International Perspective," *Daedalus: Journal of the American Academy of Arts and Sciences* (special issue on Scientific Literacy) 112, no. 2 (Spring 1983): 1–28.

4. Eric A. Hanushek, Paul E. Peterson, and Ludger Woessmann, "Teaching Math to the Talented," *Education Next* 11, no. 1 (Winter 2011), http://educationnext.org/teaching-math-to-the-talented.

5. Terry M. Moe, *Special Interest: Teachers Unions and America's Public Schools* (Washington, DC: Brookings Institution Press, 2011).

6. National Center for Education Statistics, US Department of Education, Institute of Education Sciences, http://nces.ed.gov/fastfacts/display.asp?id=91; and Lawrence M. Rudner, "Scholastic Achievement and Demographic Characteristics of Home School Students in 1998," *Education Policy Analysis Archives* 7, no. 8 (March 23, 1999), http://epaa.asu.edu/ojs/article/view/543/666.

7. Herbert J. Walberg, *School Choice: The Findings* (Washington, DC: Cato Institute, 2007). See a detailed account of studies by Caroline Hoxby, Paul Peterson, and others in this book. Of course, not every choice school excels the nearby traditional public schools.

8. Christina Clark Tuttle, Brian Gil, Philip Gleason, Virginia Knechtel, Ira Nichols-Barrer, and Alexandra Resch, "KIPP Middle Schools: Impacts on Achievement and Other Outcomes," Mathematica Policy Group, Washington, DC, February 27, 2013.

9. Center for Research on Education Outcomes, "Charter School Performance in New York City," Stanford University, 2013.

10. For a detailed account of the aspects of school history described in this section, see Herbert J. Walberg and Joseph L. Bast, *Education and Capitalism: How Overcoming Our Fear of Markets and Economics Can Improve America's Schools* (Stanford, CA: Hoover Institution Press, 2003).

11. William J. Fowler and Herbert J. Walberg, "School Size, Characteristics, and Outcomes," *Educational Evaluation and Policy Analysis* 13, no. 2 (1991): 189–202.

12. Mary Wisniewski, "Chicago School Board to Vote on Mass School Closing," *Chicago Sun-Times,* May 22, 2013.

13. James S. Coleman, "Academic Achievement and the Structure of Competition," *Harvard Education Review* 29, no. 4 (Fall 1959). Reprinted in *Education Next* 6, no. 1 (Winter 2006), http://educationnext.org/theadolescentsociety.

14. Charles L. Glenn, "The Impact of Faith-based Schools on Lives and on Society: Policy Implications" (Boston: Boston University, unpublished manuscript, n.d.).

15. Walberg, *School Choice: The Findings.*

16. Paul E. Peterson, "Impact of Choice and Competition on Student Achievement," Harvard University, unpublished conference paper, 2012.

17. James B. Stanfield, ed., *The Profit Motive in Education: Continuing the Revolution* (London: Institute of Economic Affairs, 2012).

CHAPTER 6

Implementing Standards and Testing

Williamson M. Evers

The 1983 *A Nation at Risk* report on K–12 education was a wake-up call that spoke in distressing tones about America's "once unchallenged preeminence" being "overtaken by competitors throughout the world." It used eloquent but stern and sobering language about a "rising tide of mediocrity" and the need for solid curricula and higher academic standards.[1] *A Nation at Risk* called for action by schools, local districts, and states and proposed a system of state and local standardized tests.

In the wake of *A Nation at Risk,* reformers sought to improve schools—as they had in the past—by varying and increasing inputs. Spending was increased, textbooks and other teaching materials revised, the number of academic class-offerings expanded, and graduation requirements tightened. But by the end of the 1980s, tinkering with inputs was still producing lackluster school

This paper contains considerable material from longer research projects of mine on the history of efforts at a national curriculum in America (sponsored by the Pioneer Institute) and on the history of conservatives and the public schools in America (sponsored by the Hoover Institution's Koret Task Force on K–12 Education).

performance. At that point many school reformers concluded that wholesale systemic reform was necessary.

Some of them turned to vouchers, with the belief that replacing the existing public-school monopoly with a system of competing schools would be more effective. Others turned to accountability, which would require testing to measure student mastery of explicit curriculum standards—something state governments had never done.

Standards and accountability is an approach to school reform that uses tests to monitor results. Curriculum-content standards lay out what students are expected to know, the students are tested on the material, and then an accountability system holds the various participants in the educational system responsible for students' performance.

Curriculum-content standards set forth academic content to be learned. Performance standards delineate expected levels of achievement on tests. The advocates of standards—local, state, or national—do not anticipate that the existence of content standards in and of themselves will result in higher student achievement. But they set a goal for teaching and learning, form a basis for the tests, and, in the words of historian Diane Ravitch, aim to "create a common curriculum."[2]

Systemic Reform

During the administrations of George H. W. Bush and Bill Clinton, there were several serious efforts to put into place national curriculum-content standards, national tests, or both. None of these attempts succeeded. But at the same time, a new scheme was suggested for how to construct a reform that was based on standards and accountability. "Systemic reform" was proposed in a paper by Jennifer O'Day of the American Institutes for Research and Clinton education official Marshall Smith.

O'Day and Smith contended that the constitutional responsibility of the states for public education caused a "fragmentation" of the "current policy system." This fragmentation they saw as a major obstacle to reform. (In other words, they objected to America's federal system.)

Their proposal cited the George H. W. Bush-era national standards, called for a "common content core" (with some local variations), and urged states nationwide to have aligned curriculum-content standards, tests, curriculum materials, teacher training, and in-service professional development.[3] Smith had served as chief of staff to the first US secretary of education, Shirley Hufstedler, in the Carter administration, was deputy secretary of education during the Clinton years, and was later a high official and adviser in the US Department of Education during the Obama administration.[4]

Systemic reform was, as historian Maris Vinovskis pointed out, a theory that hadn't been proven, and in addition was "difficult to implement practically."[5] As they have with many other K–12 educational reform efforts pushed by the federal government, progressive educators piggybacked their own agenda on the back of systemic reform.[6] The best illustration of this piggybacking is what happened in the Systemic Initiative of the National Science Foundation (NSF) during the 1990s.[7]

NSF's Systemic Initiative & Curriculum

Biologist Michael McKeown and his colleagues looked at the creation of the NSF's systemic initiatives and how they operated in Los Angeles and Texas. The initiatives required teaching practices (cooperative learning, discovery learning) that are not supported by a consensus of research psychologists.[8] McKeown and his colleagues found that the NSF initiatives tended to reduce academic standards for instruction in math and "weaken" the educational basis on which American science necessarily rests.[9] The math standards promoted by the NSF initiative for Los Angeles were "comical" in their shortcomings.[10]

Biologist Stan Metzenberg, in testimony before a subcommittee of the House of Representatives, said that the NSF Systemic Initiative in Los Angeles had learning expectations that were "shockingly low" for high school students. The Systemic Initiative programs nationwide were, Metzenberg said, based on sets of national science standards that were riddled with errors and relied on "post-modernist" research, in which "what is generally called a scientific fact" is instead "taken to be merely a belief system."[11] These sets of national science standards that the NSF endorsed and used for its Systemic Initiative programs were not adequate, Metzenberg said, to prepare students who might want to major in scientific fields in college.[12]

McKeown and his colleagues listed the NSF-approved textbooks for initiatives in Los Angeles and New York City. Almost all, they said, adhered to "an extreme version of discovery learning," "a constructivist philosophy," and "a radical interpretation" of the National Council of Teachers of Mathematics national math standards. These included "constant availability of calculators," beginning in kindergarten, "extreme de-emphasis" of pencil-and-paper calculation, and "de-emphasis" of "analytical and deductive methods."[13]

One of these textbook series is described as failing to include key content areas, poorly designed for learning to mastery, filled with contrived problems, and not likely to prepare students for math-based science courses or college mathematics.[14]

Standards and Accountability in the States

During the Clinton administration, systemic reform was tried at the state level as well as the national level. Different states did things differently (as one might expect in a federal system) when it came to systemic-reform's component parts: content standards, tests, curriculum materials, teacher training, and professional development. Here are a few examples, selected to show the range of what was done:

Kentucky. Education policy analyst Chester Finn described Kentucky's systemic reform as based on a "cumbersome and hyper-centralized" plan. He said that by adopting the systemic approach, Kentucky was sticking to the education establishment's party line. After considering the data on Kentucky, Finn came out against the systemic approach. He called it uniform and tightly controlled from above. He pointed out the lack of evidence that the systemic approach produces superior results.[15]

Finn called proponents of systemic reform "Hamiltonians," who believe that powerful, centralized control of education is necessary. Systemic reform, Finn said, is a fancy phrase that means "keeping power where it's always been" and managing schools in a rigid, formulaic manner.[16] Indeed, the NSF itself acknowledged that systemic reform requires districts and schools to abandon their traditional role in regulation of local schools' practices and take on a new role as "technical assisters."[17]

Kentucky followed its historic preference for this sort of centralized education policy by being the first state to adopt (sight unseen) the Common Core national curriculum-content standards.

Massachusetts. In 1993 (long before No Child Left Behind), the state dramatically increased funding of K–12 public education in return for a package of reforms. These included high curriculum-content standards and tough achievement tests for students, tough subject-matter tests for teachers, accountability for teacher-training schools, and a strong system of accountability. Massachusetts had high academic standards, accountability, and enhanced school choice. From that time until policy was reversed during the Deval Patrick administration, Massachusetts put in place a set of reforms that have, without doubt, been the most successful of any state's.

With its new curriculum, better teacher quality, demanding tests, and thorough accountability, Massachusetts's National

Assessment of Educational Progress (NAEP) scores went up dramatically. By 2007, the average fourth grader had higher achievement scores on the state math test than the average sixth grader had in 1996.[18] Massachusetts' performance had been mediocre in the past. But by 2005, students there scored highest in the nation in all four major NAEP categories (fourth- and eighth-grade reading and math). The students in the state repeated this across-the-board success in 2007, 2009, and 2011. While American students in general have middling scores, the Massachusetts students scored close to students in Japan, Korea, and Singapore in the 2008 Trends in International Mathematics and Science Study (TIMSS). Eighth graders in Massachusetts were tied for highest in the world in science.[19]

Texas. Texas rates its schools according to how well each school's students do on its statewide test. The school's students must perform well overall, and students from minority groups must also do well. The Texas system's greatest strength has been its focus since the early 1990s on accountability. Texas leaders took a long-run view of school improvement. Expectations about performance were raised step by step over the years. Thus, Texas's statewide test has not been among the most difficult, but the test has been revised over the years to make it more challenging. Evidence suggests that Texas has been able to use its accountability system to boost its students' achievement, including the achievement of its students from minority groups. Texas Governor George W. Bush proposed during his 2000 presidential campaign that he would apply the experience of Texas at the national level. This proposal became No Child Left Behind (NCLB), President Bush's signature education reform.

California. Since the late 1990s (before No Child Left Behind), California has had strong content standards, strong tests (but too-easy grading), and the usual weaknesses in teacher quality (including weak teacher training, in-service professional development, and teacher evaluations). The state also has had the usual problems in firing low-performing teachers.

Despite the fact that California adopted challenging curriculum-content standards in the late 1990s, the national systemic reform project tried to destroy them. Indeed the NSF threatened to cut off $50 million in funding for K–12 education in California if its preferences on curriculum-content standards were not followed.[20] In this example, a national effort at standards and accountability endeavored to supersede and water down a better state-level effort.

Under the California curriculum-content standards passed in the late 1990s, all demographic segments of the student population made academic improvements. Meanwhile, a large influx of immigrants led the less-educated Latino segment to rise both in absolute numbers and as a proportion of the student population. Hence, during the years from the Clinton administration to the Obama administration, overall student performance in California has been comparatively low.[21]

George W. Bush Administration

By the early 1990s, many states had started taking steps to put statewide educational standards and testing into place. But they were by no means found in every state.

While running for president in the late 1990s, George W. Bush sought to change federal policy to a focus on holding schools accountable for student performance. He said educational success should not be measured by dollars spent, but by results achieved.[22] He pointed to his education record as governor of Texas and to Texas's strong accountability system. Bush proclaimed that he was against "federalizing education," and both he and the Republican Party's national platform opposed national tests.

The George W. Bush–era reauthorization of the Elementary and Secondary Education Act was called No Child Left Behind.[23] Among other things, it called (as a condition of receiving federal money) for states to test all students in reading and mathematics every year from grades three through eight. States were expected to create their own curriculum-content standards and tests.

Each state had to have a state-created way to show that every district and school was making adequate yearly progress toward getting all students at least to grade level. NCLB required more detailed disaggregation of data by student groups, publication of that disaggregated data, and use of the data in state accountability systems. It specified sanctions for failure to make adequate progress.

Under NCLB, all states were required to participate in the National Assessment of Educational Progress (NAEP). State results on this rough yardstick, it was thought, might shame state officials who had made their curriculum-content standards, tests, and performance levels too easy.

So long as there is federal education aid, the federal government has a responsibility to see that the money is spent according to the conditions set by Congress. Thus, NCLB was a kind of performance audit of the money the federal government was spending to improve schools.[24]

As political scientist Patrick McGuinn put it, George W. Bush wanted to make certain that the liberal education establishment was held accountable for results of school programs that claimed to expand opportunities for disadvantaged children.[25]

The NCLB regime resulted in steady but modest improvement in student achievement.[26] But the law had its critics, who over time succeeded in swaying public opinion. The name of the law became toxic, but its accountability components, despite all the controversy, have remained popular.

Among NCLB's most important critics were (1) proponents of progressive education, (2) defenders of teacher autonomy, (3) defenders of local control, and (4) those who felt NCLB didn't go far enough and wanted a uniform national (but not necessarily federal) system of standards and accountability.

Even among those who originally favored NCLB, there were liberals who rapidly became disaffected with it because they believed underfunding prevented the law from succeeding.

Some progressive education proponents favored teacher autonomy. But many others wanted to have project-based items on national tests because such items would encourage teachers to use discovery-learning teaching techniques in the classroom.[27]

Defenders of teacher autonomy wanted public schools to trust teachers' professional skills. If given the resources, defenders of autonomy said, teachers would do the job. They did not approve of looking over teachers' shoulders via tests and accountability systems. Checking up in this fashion was an insult to teacher professionalism and would interfere with teachers doing their job. Failure to trust teachers, they said, would drive the best ones out of the profession.

Many defenders of local control thought No Child Left Behind constituted federal overreach that inhibited school districts' potential. Ideally, each local school district would offer what is most wanted by those who live there. If the district did not, as economist Eugenia Toma put it, voters would "collectively vote out the school committee" or individual families would move into other districts.[28]

Lastly, proponents of national standards saw variation among the states when it came to curriculum-content standards, tests, and performance standards.[29] They saw such variation as chaos. They feared that individual state decision-making would lead inexorably to a "race to the bottom" in what states expected of students. They wanted uniformity and homogeneity.

Proponents of national standards argued that it would be valuable to be able to compare a student in Portland, Maine, to one in Portland, Oregon. They saw economies of scale in a national market for teaching materials and liked the idea of making it easier for schoolchildren to move seamlessly from state to state.

Of the many liberals who believed that NCLB was underfunded, some in the policy elite during the George W. Bush and Obama administrations thought that, once established, national standards would constitute a predicate for "adequate"—that is, vastly increased—federal funding.[30]

To understand how the Common Core national standards and accompanying tests came to be, one first has to look at the organized drive for the standards and then at the process of creating them.

The Common Core national standards began in 2006, not with the deliberations of state legislatures, but in a series of private meetings of long-time national standards advocates—some of whose advocacy dated back to the George H. W. Bush and Clinton eras.[31]

In 2007, the Council of Chief State School Officers (CCSSO) and the National Governors Association (NGA) Center for Best Practices joined the national standards effort.

One reason why some governors joined in was to suppress competition from other states. For example, Georgia (which had its own content standards and its own test) was performing poorly compared to, for example, Massachusetts (which had its own different, higher standards and test).[32] Georgia officials might well have believed that it would be to their state's advantage to use a federally supported cartel of states to suppress Massachusetts's standards and test and substitute national standards and tests that would apply to states across the country.

Indeed, states like Georgia already had an objective measure for interstate comparison in NAEP and could have used that as a yardstick. They could have each used their own state-level standards and tests together with other school-reform programs to compete on NAEP (or other measures) in accordance with America's system of competitive federalism. Instead, forty-five states and the District of Columbia turned to a federally supported cartel that, critics of Common Core claim, suppresses competition and has replaced exemplars of excellence with uniform mediocrity.

Nationalizing standards and tests would, according to this analysis, eliminate them as differentiated school-reform instruments that could be used by states in competition over educational attainment among the states. Sonny Perdue, then governor of Georgia, did not like it when the low-performing students of his state were compared with students in other states that had different standards from Georgia's. He became the lead governor in bringing the NGA into the national standards effort.[33] (In 2013, the NGA acted in similar fashion to create a cartel of states in order to suppress competitive federalism and make online retailers collect taxes from out-of-state customers.[34])

The advocacy and lobbying arms of the state schools chiefs and the governors were vital to the strategy of national-standards proponents. Their efforts were already underway before any trade associations representing the interests of state officials were on board. But now the proponents could describe their initiative as "state-led."[35]

Back in January 1995, during the reaction against the national history standards, two governors who supported national standards ruled out federal creation in the future. Gov. Roy Romer of Colorado advocated using a privately financed and operated group to create future national standards. Gov. James B. Hunt Jr. of North Carolina called for moving the creation of national standards away from the federal government. The conclusion these governors reached in 1995 became the strategy of national-standards proponents, including Romer and Hunt, in 2006 and 2007, as groundwork was laid for the Common Core national standards.[36]

The nonprofit advocacy and consulting firm Achieve Inc. played a central role in the run-up to, and creation of, the standards. Achieve was founded in 1996 by the National Governors Association[37] and some corporate leaders to work with state school superintendents on curriculum-content standards, graduation requirements, tests, and accountability systems.[38]

The governors' trade association wanted to ensure that states could have high-quality standards of their own. At the time, Achieve did not support national standards. Indeed, when the NGA created Achieve, the NGA specified that Achieve would not certify or approve any standards. In particular, it would "not endorse, develop, or financially support the development of national education standards."[39]

After more than a decade of sticking to its original assignment of working only on state standards and testing, Achieve's activities shifted to efforts that were precursors of national standards.

In Achieve's 2008 report, *Benchmarking for Success* (co-sponsored by the National Governors Association and the Council of Chief State School Officers), Achieve called for states to follow the path taken by Germany, where the federal government had recently supported a thorough centralization of curriculum-content standards and testing.[40] The report called for the US federal government to play an "enabling role" in having the states adopt "a common core" of K–12 standards in math and English.[41] By mid-2008, Achieve began to devote its energies to the creation of national curriculum-content standards and tests.

Achieve had been leading a network of states which had some of their content-standards in common. But now it rolled its efforts in this area into the Common Core initiative and provided assistance to the Common Core writing team. Although there was no direct federal involvement in the writing process itself, the standards were endorsed by the federal government and became the basis of federally funded and sponsored tests.

The George W. Bush administration encouraged states to put in place state-level standards, testing, and accountability. It extended NAEP to all states to allow for comparisons, but did not pursue national standards and tests. That policy was about to change.

Barack Obama Administration

Barack Obama did not promise national standards when he campaigned for president. But when results of the 2009 Programme for International Student Assessment (PISA) test were released, they showed that the United States was mediocre in mathematics, while students in Shanghai performed dramatically better. Both President Obama and education policy analyst Chester Finn said that these results were as important and stunning as the launching of Sputnik.[42]

The Obama administration had begun to espouse the national standards initiative, in long-time education journalist Robert Rothman's words, "soon after taking office." Education Secretary Arne Duncan and his senior counselor Marshall Smith had been advocates of national standards before they were appointed by President Obama.[43]

The Obama administration soon developed an ambitious program of federally guided K–12 education reform consisting of national curriculum-content standards and national tests based on these curriculum standards.

Thwarting an Inexorable Race to the Bottom?

Central to the Obama administration's thinking (and rhetoric) on education reform was the idea that state performance standards were already on a downward slide and that, without federal intervention, they would inexorably continue on a "race to the bottom."[44] The name given to the administration's signature school reform effort, the Race to the Top program (RttT), reflects this belief. The idea is that to prevent states from following their supposed natural dynamic of a race to the bottom,[45] the federal government needs to step in and lead a race to the top.

Critics disagree,[46] arguing that state education policymakers need to take into account not only the challenge teachers and school administrators face from rigorous content and performance standards, but also the damage that low standards would bring to the state's reputation for having a trained workforce and the damage to the policymakers' own reputations.

In 2007, the Thomas B. Fordham Institute looked empirically at state performance standards over time in a study called *The*

Proficiency Illusion. The study showed that while states had a variety of performance standards (as would be expected in a federal system), the race to the bottom was not happening.[47]

Race to the Top

To finance Race to the Top, the US Department of Education took discretionary stimulus money that could be used as conditional grants, and then turned a portion of that money into a competitive grant program. It used the grants to encourage states to adopt the national standards. Policy analyst Michael Petrilli aptly called inducements to adopt the standards "the carrot that feels like a stick."[48] The department also paid for national consortia to develop national tests aligned with the national curriculum-content standards.

NCLB Waivers

The administration created another inducement in the form of No Child Left Behind waivers. In return for adopting the national standards or a federally approved alternative, states could escape NCLB sanctions for not making timely gains in student achievement.[49] Critics said that Secretary Duncan was going beyond what the law allows by substituting the Obama administration's favored education reforms (including national curriculum-content standards and tests) for NCLB's accountability measures. Critics also pointed out that the new accountability systems under the waivers may hide deficiencies in the performance of children in previously closely watched sub-groups and may weaken incentives to improve performance of those children.[50]

In addition, some of the substantive policy changes the Obama administration wants to put in place—through RttT and the conditional waivers—are in the area of a national curriculum.[51] Yet three federal statutes prohibit the Education Department from making policy on curriculum.[52]

Quality of the Common Core National Standards

The new national academic-content standards for English and math are no better than the standards in place in one quarter of the states and weaker than those in a half-dozen states.[53] Though they are certainly a step up for many states, there was no effort to accommodate states that prior to 2010 had standards that were better than Common Core.[54]

Adoption of the Common Core

The Obama administration used the fine print in its Race to the Top scoring rubric to ensure that there would be only one set of national standards. States would be in a better competitive position if they adopted a "common set of K–12 standards" that had been adopted by "a majority of the states."[55] By definition, if a majority of states is needed, there can be only one set that is adopted. Any set adopted by a minority would put a state that adopted it at a distinct disadvantage. Hence, there came to be only one set of national standards.

After the Common Core State Standards Initiative (CCSSI) issued its standards in June 2010, the Department of Education insisted that states that wanted to compete effectively for Race to the Top grants had to adopt national standards by August. The standards were written in a hurry to meet federal deadlines and were never piloted in a state or locality. Kentucky (where Gene Wilhoit, at the time the executive director of the Common Core–sponsoring Council of Chief State School Officers, had recently been state commissioner of education) adopted the new national standards sight unseen in February 2010, months ahead of their publication.[56]

Thus, during 2010 and 2011, forty-five states plus the District of Columbia adopted the Common Core national curriculum-content standards.[57] The federal government is paying for the creation of national assessments and encouraging states to use them to fulfill NCLB requirements for testing and accountability. The federal government also set criteria for the design of the assessments and has established a federal technical review board to oversee the design.[58]

National Tests

In September 2010, the Department of Education awarded $330 million for the creation of national tests. Both the testing consortia that received federal grants included commitments in their proposals that they would develop national curriculum materials. Key writers of the national standards were subsequently retained to develop the national tests.[59]

Progressive educators, particularly advocates of "authentic assessment" and "performance-based assessment," had been hoping to use national tests to influence the curriculum.[60] They envisioned project-based tests that use "open-ended performances in which students develop solutions, write explanations, or evaluate potential strategies."[61]

At least a portion of the test problems will be project-based, designed to evaluate such skills as "complex problem-solving" and communication.[62] Such testing is intended to encourage the use of discovery-learning techniques in the classroom.

Stanford Education Professor Linda Darling-Hammond, a longtime proponent of progressive teaching methods, was a prominent spokeswoman for the Obama campaign in 2008. She is widely credited with being the intellectual leader of the Smarter Balanced Assessment Consortium, which was awarded one of the two contracts to create national tests.

Darling-Hammond praises "good language" in the Common Core national curriculum-content standards about critical thinking skills and problem-solving. In a 2011 interview by Lynnette Guastaferro of *Teaching Matters*, Darling-Hammond says that whether the national standards are put into effect in a way that is "much more focused on higher-order learning skills" (that is, progressive education classrooms for all) depends on "building curriculum materials," "transforming" testing, and changing in-service teacher training.

Darling-Hammond says it is "especially important," if you want to remake American public education, to "rethink" testing. Other countries, she says, do not make extensive use of multiple-choice questions. Instead, they test primarily in "open-ended formats" with "performances" and "projects" as part of the examination system. Her assessment consortium will "move the needle" in the direction of what she considers "more thoughtful" tests.[63]

Common Core–aligned textbooks and teacher professional development do, as of this writing, seem to be fulfilling Darling-Hammond's vision of a nationwide turn toward inquiry-based learning.

Critics of the national tests maintain that what is tested is what is taught and that the combination of national tests, national standards, RttT grants, and NCLB waivers puts America on the road to a national curriculum. Most national standards and testing proponents counter that states and districts may still select their own teaching materials and devise their own lesson plans.

State of the Current Research

States that were early adopters of standards and accountability after the passage of No Child Left Behind saw achievement gains.[64] During the George W. Bush administration, there were modest but steady gains induced by standards and accountability. There was no race to the bottom in performance standards.

It is not yet possible to measure the new generation of national standards and tests. But we can (1) look around the world to countries that do and do not have national standards, (2) look at whether standards that are already in place have reduced whatever variation can be reduced, (3) ask whether Common Core has the look and feel of standards in high-performing countries, and

(4) compare Common Core to Bush-era state standards and those of high-performing countries.

Looking at other countries, there is no reason to believe that a national curriculum leads to better results. For example, some countries that are culturally similar to the United States and set their curriculum at the provincial level—such as Australia and Canada—do better academically than the United States. Other countries with cultures similar to the United States that set their curriculum at the national level—such as Denmark and France— do not do particularly well.[65]

Brookings Institution education researcher Tom Loveless has looked at whether the Common Core will boost student achievement. He concludes in the 2012 Brown Center Report on American Education that there will be "little or no impact" on how much children learn.

Loveless uses California as an example. He points out that California has had:

- State curriculum frameworks since at least 1962
- Statewide testing with scores for every school published publicly since 1971 (except for a brief timeout in the early 1990s)
- State K–8 textbook adoption since the nineteenth century
- A court-ordered equalized spending system since the late 1970s[66]

Loveless notes that any effects such standards-based policies might have on decreasing variation in achievement within California have already happened.[67]

Loveless adds that every state has tremendous within-state variation in performance. "Every state," Loveless says, "including Massachusetts and Mississippi," has a high-performing mini-Massachusetts and a low-performing mini-Mississippi range of learning within its borders. "That variation," he says, "will go untouched" by the Common Core.[68]

William Schmidt, a mathematics-education researcher at Michigan State University who looked at the Common Core math standards and math standards in high-performing countries, reported great similarity in the number of standards and in their form.[69] One of his critics, former US Department of Education official Ze'ev Wurman, said the Common Core math standards list more topics than do the standards in the high-performing countries. Wurman also said Common Core follows a different sequence than that in high-performing countries.[70]

The Thomas B. Fordham Institute reviewed the Common Core math standards and judged them clearer and more challenging than most (but not all) the state standards they replaced. At the same time, it found that the Common Core math standards are less rigorous than the best state math standards (those in California, the District of Columbia, Florida, Indiana, and Washington).

Although writers of the Common Core math standards looked at standards in the highest-performing countries, they did not match what is expected in those countries. R. James Milgram, a retired Stanford mathematics professor, described Common Core math (by the end of seventh grade) as "roughly two years behind" high-achieving countries.[71] Milgram is echoed by Jonathan Goodman, a mathematics professor at the Courant Institute at New York University.[72]

At the 2010 annual conference of mathematics societies, University of Arizona Professor William McCallum, one of the three principal writers of the Common Core mathematics standards, said they are not particularly high, "certainly not in comparison [with] other nations, including East Asia, where math education excels."[73]

On the other hand, Edward Frenkel and Hung-Hsi Wu, of the Department of Mathematics at the University of California, Berkeley, point out that the Common Core has good ideas on how to teach fractions and assert the "race to the bottom" thesis. They say the only way to combat America's "current lock-step march to the bottom" of international achievement in math and science is to put national standards in place.[74]

Regardless of whether Common Core improves student achievement, it will change the face of American education and substantially shift the locus of control from the states and localities to Washington, DC.[75]

Avenues for Future Research

There are avenues for future research at both the macro and micro levels of education policy. Some of the possible research at micro levels is particularly important because it is at the micro level that teachers and administrators put education policy into practice.

Because of the NCLB waivers, there is a myriad of new research challenges in the field of accountability. At the macro level: What kind of results will the new practice of setting different annual expected gains for different student groups yield? What will be the effect on the success of groups that in the past have been low-performing? Will the NCLB spotlight that used to shine on such groups of students be turned off? At the micro level, will the complex new accountability systems created by waiver states be transparent enough and understandable enough for teachers, parents, principals, and journalists? Will these systems, as the Center on Education Policy wondered in 2012, "create an environment for subterfuge and make it easier for states to mask poor academic performance"?[76]

The Common Core national standards are, as of this writing, being put into effect across the United States. The national tests produced by the consortia have not been administered, although items have been field-tested.

Many Common Core topics are worthy of research. At the micro level, case studies can look at how schools handle the requirement that students read more informational texts. How will science, history, and social science classes deliver on this requirement of the national English standards? How well will English teachers deliver on it as well? How well will comprehension of informational texts be tested?

At the micro level, how well will students learn similar and congruent triangles in classes that follow the Common Core prescription of using the idea of rigid motion (an approach that is experimental for K–12 education) to teach this topic? How will the Common Core affect textbooks and other teaching materials? How will it affect classroom teaching techniques?

Researchers can perform content analysis of the new national tests and other tests (SAT, ACT, Advanced Placement, and others) said to be aligned with the Common Core. For example, a recent Common Core–aligned English test has been scrutinized in North Carolina.[77] Researchers are just beginning to look at recently published results for Common Core–aligned tests in New York and Kentucky. Comparative content analysis of tests in Common Core and non-Common Core states can be carried out.

Another research topic is macro-level comparative analysis of student achievement in Common Core and non-Common Core states. Although imperfect, the National Assessment of Educational Progress and the testing system of the Northwest Evaluation Association are probably the best available yardsticks. Given the coverage of social-science topics in the Common Core national English standards, it is unfortunate that the NAEP governing board has recently removed some of these important yardsticks: its fourth-grade and eighth-grade tests for civics, history, and geography, as well as its high school transcript study that could have provided early indications of Common Core's impacts.[78]

There can be studies of the effect of Common Core on Catholic and other private schools. In particular, will national uniformity of curriculum under Common Core crowd out uniquely Catholic characteristics? The effect on charter schools should also be evaluated.[79] In particular, will progressive education aspects of the national standards and tests harm "no excuses" charters (which stress mastery of content by students from weak educational backgrounds)?[80]

Before-and-after studies of performance can be conducted in Common Core states, including those with previous comparatively high performance (like Massachusetts) and those in the medium- or low-performing range.

The transition from testing state standards to testing national standards may be abrupt in most states. For evaluation purposes, it would be better to have students take both tests for a while, but this is unlikely because of the expense and time required.

In sum, the arrival of the Common Core is one of the biggest changes in the history of American education. It will generate a considerable number of topics for research and analysis.

Notes

1. National Commission on Excellence in Education, *A Nation at Risk: The Imperative for Educational Reform* (Washington, DC: US Department of Education, 1983), 5–8.

2. Diane Ravitch, *EdSpeak: A Glossary of Educational Terms, Phrases, Buzzwords, and Jargon* (Alexandria, VA: Association for Supervision and Curriculum Development, 2007), 58.

3. Jennifer A. O'Day and Marshall S. Smith, "Systemic Reform and Educational Opportunity," in *Designing Coherent Education Policy: Improving the System*, ed. Susan H. Fuhrman (San Francisco: Jossey-Bass, 1993), 250, 265–69, 300n.2; see also Chester E. Finn Jr., *Troublemaker: A Personal History of School Reform since Sputnik* (Princeton, NJ: Princeton University Press, 2008), 150–51; and Maris A. Vinovskis, *From A Nation at Risk to No Child Left Behind: National Education Goals and the Creation of Federal Education Policy* (New York: Teachers College Press, 2009), 58, 68–69.

4. Melinda Malico, "Marshall (Mike) S. Smith Retires (Again) from ED," *Homeroom* (blog), US Department of Education,

May 26, 2010, http://www.ed.gov/blog/2010/05/marshall
-mike-s-smith-ph-d-retires-again-from-ed.

5. Vinovskis, *From* A Nation at Risk, 215.

6. Chester E. Finn Jr. described progressive educators' actions as a "hijacking." See Chester E. Finn Jr., "Who's Afraid of the Big, Bad Test?" in *Debating the Future of American Education: Do We Need National Standards and Assessments?*, ed. Diane Ravitch (Washington, DC: Brookings Institution Press, 1995), 143n.4. These actions are best described as piggybacking, not hijacking, since O'Day and Smith endorse learning "complex problem-solving skills," the 1989 NCTM national math standards, and NSF's Systemic State Initiative. O'Day and Smith, "Systemic Reform," 263, 264, 296, 298, 299n.2.

7. On the historical background of the NSF systemic initiatives, see Michael McKeown, David Klein, and Chris Patterson, "The National Science Foundation Systemic Initiatives: How a Small Amount of Federal Money Promotes Ill-Designed Mathematics and Science Programs in K–12 and Undermines Local Control of Education," in *What's at Stake in the K–12 Standards Wars: A Primer for Educational Policy Makers*, ed. Sandra Stotsky (New York: Peter Lang, 2000), 316.

8. Ibid, 320–23, 357.

9. Ibid., 313, 281, 307n.14.

10. Ibid., 333–35.

11. Stan Metzenberg, *Testimony before the Subcommittee on Basic Research, Committee on Science, US House of Representatives*, July 23, 1998, http://web.archive.org/web/20120206165912 /http://mathematicallycorrect.com/stanmetz.htm. See also Vinovskis, *From* A Nation at Risk, 116.

12. *Follow-Up Questions for Dr. Stan Metzenberg*, http://web .archive.org/web/20120206165942/http://mathematicallycorrect .com/moremetz.htm.

13. McKeown et al., "Systemic Initiatives," 324.

14. Ibid., 326.

15. Chester E. Finn Jr., "Bad Grades; Good Idea," *Weekly Standard*, February 10, 1997, 17–18.

16. Chester E. Finn Jr., "Reforming Education: A Whole New World," *First Things,* May 1997.

17. Quoted in McKeown et al., "Systemic Initiatives," 355.

18. Charles D. Chieppo and James T. Gass, "Accountability Overboard," *Education Next* 9, no. 2 (Spring 2009), 18.

19. James Stergios, Charles Chieppo, and Jamie T. Gass, "The Massachusetts Exception," *City Journal* 22, no. 3 (Summer 2012), 82.

20. McKeown et al., "Systemic Initiatives," 332–33, 357–59.

21. Richard Innes, "Kentucky's Common Core Data a Warning to the Nation," interview on *Girard at Large,* radio program, August 6, 2013, http://www.girardatlarge.com/2013/08 /kentuckys-common-core-data-a-warning-to-the-nation.

22. George W. Bush, *Decision Points* (New York: Crown Publishers, 2011), 274.

23. No Child Left Behind Act of 2001, Pub. Law 107–110, 115 Stat. 1425; see also Vinovskis, *From* A Nation at Risk, 169–70.

24. See George W. Bush, *A Fresh Start for America: Policy Addresses of George W. Bush* (Bush for President, 1999), 10, 15–16, 23, 41.

25. Patrick J. McGuinn, *No Child Left Behind and the Transformation of Federal Education Policy, 1965–2005* (Lawrence: University Press of Kansas, 2006), 157. On the similar attitude of many congressional Republicans, see ibid., 172.

26. Paul E. Peterson, "What Do the Latest NAEP Scores Tell Us About NCLB?" *Education Next,* November 7, 2011, http:// educationnext.org/what-do-the-latest-naep-scores-tell-us-about -nclb/; and Thomas Dee and Brian A. Jacob, "Evaluating NCLB," *Education Next* 10, no. 3 (Summer 2010), 54.

27. Robert Rothman, *Something in Common: The Common Core Standards and the Next Chapter in American Education* (Cambridge, MA: Harvard Education Press, 2011), 6.

28. Eugenia Froedge Toma, "Education," in *Agenda for Progress: Examining Federal Spending,* ed. Eugene J. McAllister (Washington, DC: Heritage Foundation,1981), 197, 200;

see also Charles M. Tiebout, "A Pure Theory of Local Expenditure," *Journal of Political Economy* 64, no. 5 (October 1956), 416.

29. McGuinn, *Transformation of Federal Education Policy,* 192–93; and John Cronin, Michael Dahlin, Yun Xiang, and Donna McCahon, "The Accountability Illusion," Thomas B. Fordham Institute, February 2009, http://www.edexcellence .net/publications/the-accountability-illusion.html.

30. For example: "It makes no sense to expect schools, districts, and states to reach national student achievement goals, if their financial resources . . . are unequal. . . . If we are to adopt and raise national standards for education, the nation must as well increase its commitment to equality through increased and equitable financial investments. . . ." See Cindy Brown and Elena Rocha, "The Case for National Standards, Accountability, and Fiscal Equity," Center for American Progress, November 8, 2005, 4, 7.

31. Rothman, *Something in Common,* 53.

32. Although the 2004 Georgia Performance Standards were higher in curriculum-content expectations than those in many states, they were not as high as those in Massachusetts. However, during 2009-2011, Georgia lowered its expectations of student performance on state tests more than any other state in the country. Paul E. Peterson and Peter Kaplan, "Despite Common Core, States Still Lack Common Standards," *Education Next* 13, no. 4 (Fall 2013), 45, 49, http://educationnext.org /despite-common-core-states-still-lack-common-standards.

33. Dane Linn, "The Role of Governors," in *Common Core Meets Education Reform: What It All Means for Politics, Policy, and the Future of Schooling,* ed. Frederick M. Hess and Michael Q. McShane (New York: Teachers College Press, 2013), 39. The Georgia Public Policy Foundation writes: "Common Core . . . brought at least 37 state standards into close alignment with Georgia. This critical mass means tests, textbooks and other instructional materials are now likely to be more closely aligned with Georgia's standards." See "Background and

Analysis of the Common Core State Standards As They Relate to Georgia" (Atlanta: Georgia Public Policy Foundation, August 2013), 12. See also Bill Crane, "Sonny Perdue's Non-Legacy," *Georgia Trend*, January 2011, http://www.georgiatrend.com /January-2011/Georgia-View-Sonny-Perdues-Non-Legacy; also, Reid Wilson, "The Republican Case for Common Core," *GovBeat* (blog), *Washington Post,* August 23, 2013, http:// www.washingtonpost.com/blogs/govbeat/wp/2013/08/23 /the-republican-case-for-common-core.

34. Grover Norquist, president of Americans for Tax Reform, said, "The genius of America is to have the fifty states compete to provide the best government at the lowest cost. The NGA is fighting to establish a cartel in order to avoid competition which would lead to better, less expensive government." Quoted in John Kartch, "In Push for Internet Sales Tax, NGA Accuses Its Chairman of Presiding Over a 'Tax Haven,'" Americans for Tax Reform (news release), April 26, 2013, http://www.atr.org /push-internet-sales-tax-nga-accuses-a7573.

35. Rothman, *Something in Common,* 56, 57. A 2008 Achieve report explained the reason for this strategy: "Federal efforts to influence—let alone direct or determine—state standards have met with stiff and effective political resistance." See Achieve Report, "Out of Many, One: Toward Rigorous Common Core Standards from the Ground Up," July 31, 2008, http://www .achieve.org/files/OutofManyOne.pdf.

36. See also Roy Romer, in Alliance for Excellent Education briefing on "Something in Common," October 18, 2011, video at 69.03-70.21 minutes, http://media.all4ed.org/briefing -oct-18-2011. Compare Roy Romer, "Explaining Standards to the Public," in *Debating the Future,* 66–68.

37. The National Governors Association is a trade association that engages in public advocacy, lobbying, and policy development in line with the interests of governors. See http://www.nga.org /cms/about.

38. See Achieve website, http://www.achieve.org/about-us, and "Achieve & The American Diploma Project Network," http://

www.achieve.org/files/About%20AchieveADP-Apr2012.pdf. See also Barbara O. Pilling, "A Critical Analysis of the Modern Standards Movement: A Historical Portrayal Through Archival Review, Written Documents, and Oral Testimony from 1983 to 1995" (doctoral dissertation, Virginia Polytechnic Institute and State University, April 1999), 70, http://scholar.lib.vt.edu/theses /available/etd-041899-145816/unrestricted/PartI.pdf; and Vinovskis, From A Nation at Risk, 133–34.

39. Millicent Lawton, "NGA Approves Group to Aid in Standards-Setting Efforts," *Education Week*, May 29, 1996; and Millicent Lawton, "Governors OK 'Entity' to Oversee Standards," *Education Week*, August 7, 1996. For the ban on work on national standards, see Vinovskis, *From* A Nation At Risk, 103.

40. National Governors Association, Council of Chief State School Officers, and Achieve Inc., "Benchmarking for Success: Ensuring US Students Receive a World-Class Education," December 2008, 16, 37.

41. Ibid., 6–7.

42. Ibid., 8.

43. Malico, "Marshall (Mike) S. Smith Retires (Again)."

44. Brown and Rocha, "The Case for National Standards," 1; and Vinovskis, *From* A Nation at Risk, 219.

45. For critics of the supposed natural dynamic of a "race to the bottom" in policy fields other than education, see Jonathan H. Adler, "Interstate Competition and the Race to the Top," *Harvard Journal of Law and Public Policy* 35, no. 1 (March 2, 2012), 89, 96–97; Scott R. Saleska and Kirsten H. Engel, "'Facts Are Stubborn Things': An Empirical Reality Check in the Theoretical Debate Over the Race-to-the-Bottom in State Environmental Standard-Setting," *Cornell Journal of Law and Public Policy* 8 (1998), 55–86; and John Ferejohn and Barry R. Weingast, eds., *The New Federalism: Can The States Be Trusted?* (Stanford, CA: Hoover Institution Press, 1997).

46. Adler, "Interstate Competition"; Saleska and Engel, "'Facts Are Stubborn Things'"; and Ferejohn and Weingast, *The New Federalism*.

47. See Chester E. Finn Jr. and Michael J. Petrilli, foreword to John Cronin, Michael Dahlin, Deborah Adkins, and G. Gage Kingsbury, "The Proficiency Illusion," Thomas B. Fordham Institute, October 2007, 4, http://www.edexcellence.net /publications/theproficiencyillusion.html. This study and a 2009 Fordham study, "The Accountability Illusion," stressed that this variety of performance standards (that would be expected in a federal system) meant that a school that was deemed to be doing well in Mississippi would probably not be deemed to be doing well in Massachusetts. In 1997, the Clinton administration made equivalent claims of a race to the bottom in its time. See John F. Jennings, *Why National Standards and Tests? Politics and the Quest for Better Schools* (Thousand Oaks, CA: SAGE Publications, 1998), 177–78.

48. Michael J. Petrilli, "The Race to the Top: The Carrot That Feels Like a Stick," *Flypaper* (blog), Thomas B. Fordham Institute, July 23, 2009, http://www.edexcellence.net/commentary /education-gadfly-daily/flypaper/2009/the-race-to-the-top-the -carrot-that-feels-like-a-stick.html. Petrilli was primarily referring to the detailed requirements.

49. On issuing of waivers as a serious problem for the rule of law, see Richard A. Epstein, "Government by Waiver," *National Affairs* (Spring 2011), 39. Epstein is writing about the effect of waivers by all levels of government on private firms and individuals, but much of what he says applies also to federal waivers granted to states, local governments, and school districts.

50. Michele McNeil, "Ed. Trust Slams NCLB Waivers for Neglecting At-Risk Students," *Politics K–12* (blog), *Education Week,* February 7, 2013, http://blogs.edweek.org/edweek /campaign-K–12/2013/02/ed_trust_slams_nclb_waivers_fo.html.

51. The Obama administration said in its blueprint for reauthorization of the Elementary and Secondary Education Act that it wanted adoption of common college- and career-readiness standards or a federally approved alternative to be a required condition for states to receive federal aid to education under Title I of ESEA. See "A Blueprint for Reform: The

Reauthorization of the Elementary and Secondary Education Act" (Washington, DC: US Department of Education, March 2010), 3, http://www2.ed.gov/policy/elsec/leg/blueprint /blueprint.pdf.

52. Robert S. Eitel, Kent D. Talbert, and Williamson M. Evers, "The Road to a National Curriculum: The Legal Aspects of the Common Core Standards, Race to the Top, and Conditional Waivers," Pioneer Institute, February 2012.

53. Sheila Byrd Carmichael, W. Stephen Wilson, Kathleen Porter-Magee, and Gabrielle Martino, "The State of State Standards—and the Common Core—in 2010." The study was published in July 2010 by the Thomas B. Fordham Institute and supported in part by the Gates Foundation, http://www.edexcellence.net /publications/the-state-of-state-of-standards-and-the-common -core-in-2010.html.

54. Liam Julian wrote in 2009, "Several states have actually managed to craft admirable standards, among them California, Indiana, and Massachusetts; and several others are revising standards that badly need it. Will these states be compelled to jettison the results of their fine work and remake their curricula and assessments to jibe with 'voluntary' national standards?" See Liam Julian, "Against National Standards," *Weekly Standard* 14, no. 44 (August 10, 2009), https://www .weeklystandard.com/Content/Public/Articles/000/000 /016/795coxmj.asp.

55. Federal Register, "Overview Information; Race to the Top Fund; Notice Inviting Applications for New Awards for Fiscal Year (FY) 2010." See Appendix B, Reviewer Guidance Specific to (B)(2)(ii)—Significant Number of States, http://www2 .ed.gov/programs/racetothetop/scoringrubric.pdf. I am indebted to Ze'ev Wurman for this point.

56. Rothman, *Something in Common*, 71–72, 101–102.

57. Catherine Gewertz, "Common-Standards Watch: Montana Makes 47," *Curriculum Matters* (blog), *Education Week*, November 4, 2011, http://blogs.edweek.org/edweek/curriculum /2011/11/common-standards_watch_montana.html.

58. Catherine Gewertz, "Common-Assessment Groups to Undergo New Federal Review Process," *Curriculum Matters* (blog), *Education Week,* April, 1, 2013, http://blogs.edweek.org Catherine /edweek/curriculum/2013/04/common_assessment _groups_to_undergo_new_federal_review_process.html.

59. Rothman, *Something in Common,* 28.

60. This is similar to efforts during the Clinton administration to use NSF-funded teaching materials as a basis for a progressive education curriculum. See McKeown et al., "Systemic Initiatives," 332–33, 357–59.

61. Lauren B. Resnick, Mary Kay Stein, and Sarah Coon, "Standards-Based Reform: A Powerful Idea Unmoored," in *Improving on No Child Left Behind: Getting Education Reform Back on Track,* ed. Richard D. Kahlenberg (New York: The Century Foundation, 2008), 103, 131–32.

62. McKeown et al., "Systemic Initiatives," 29. On Gates Foundation support for project-based testing tied to the Common Core national-curriculum standards, see Vicki Phillips and Carina Wong, "Tying Together the Common Core of Standards, Instruction, and Assessments," *Phi Delta Kappan* 91, no. 5 (February 2010), 40–42. I am indebted to Ze'ev Wurman for this reference.

63. Lynnette Guastaferro, "A Conversation with Linda Darling-Hammond," *Teaching Matters* (blog), October 19, 2011, http://www.teachingmatters.org/blog/conversation-linda -darling-hammond. On Linda Darling-Hammond's research on the effect of teaching credentials, see Kate Walsh, "Teacher Certification Reconsidered: Stumbling for Quality" (Baltimore: The Abell Foundation, 2001).

64. Nancy Kober, Naomi Chudowsky, and Victor Chudowsky, "Has Student Achievement Increased Since 2002? State Test Score Trends Through 2006–07," Center on Education Policy, 2008.

65. Grover J. "Russ" Whitehurst, "Don't Forget Curriculum," Brown Center Letters on Education, no. 3 (October 2009), http://www.brookings.edu/papers/2009/1014_curriculum

_whitehurst.aspx; and Neal McCluskey, "Behind the Curtain: Assessing the Case for National Curriculum Standards," Cato Institute Policy Analysis no. 661 (February 17, 2010), http://www.cato.org/pub_display.php?pub_id=11217.

66. See Tom Loveless, "Predicting the Effect of Common Core State Standards on Student Achievement," in "The 2012 Brown Center Report on American Education: How Well are American Students Learning?" 3, no. 1, Brookings Institution Press (February 2012), 6, 12–13, http://www.brookings.edu/~/media /Files/rc/reports/2012/0216_brown_education_loveless/0216 _brown_education_loveless.pdf.

67. Ibid., 13.

68. Ibid., 12.

69. William Schmidt, "Seizing the Moment for Mathematics," *Education Week,* July 18, 2012, http://www.edweek.org/ew /articles/2012/07/18/36schmidt.h31.html.

70. Ze'ev Wurman, "Math Commentary Doesn't Add Up," *Education Week,* August 8, 2012, http://www.edweek.org/ew /articles/2012/08/08/37letters-4.h31.html; and Ze'ev Wurman, "Why Math Standards Don't Measure Up," Pioneer Institute web log, June 24, 2013 http://pioneerinstitute.org/news/why -common-cores-math-standards-dont-measure-up-by-guest -blogger-zeev-wurman.

71. "James Milgram on the New Core Curriculum Standards in Math," *Parents Across America* (blog), April 17, 2011, http://parentsacrossamerica.org/james-milgram-on-the-new-core -curriculum-standards-in-math/. See also R. James Milgram, "Review of the Final Draft Core Standards," in Sandra Stotsky and Ze'ev Wurman, "Common Core's Standards Still Don't Make the Grade: Why Massachusetts and California Must Regain Control Over Their Academic Destinies," Pioneer Institute White Paper no. 65 (Boston: Pioneer Institute, July 2010), 42 (p. 3 of appendix), http://pioneerinstitute.org /download/common-cores-standards-still-dont-make-the-grade.

72. Jonathan Goodman, "A Comparison of Proposed US Common Core Math Standard to Standards of Selected Asian Countries,"

Education News, July 9, 2010, http://www.educationnews.org /ed_reports/94979.html.

73. Ze'ev Wurman and W. Stephen Wilson, "The Common Core Math Standards," *Education Next* 12, no. 3 (Summer 2012), 44, http://educationnext.org/the-common-core-math -standards.

74. Edward Frenkel and Hung-Hsi Wu, "Republicans Should Love 'Common Core'," *Wall Street Journal,* May 6, 2013, http://online.wsj.com/article /SB10001424127887324482504578453502155934978.html.

75. Robert Scott, "A Republic of Republics: How Common Core Undermines State and Local Autonomy over K–12 Education," Pioneer Institute, September 2013.

76. Wayne Riddle and Nancy Kober, "Accountability Issues to Watch under NCLB Waivers," Center on Education Policy, October 2, 2012.

77. Terry Stoops, "Goodbye, Grammar: N.C.'s Common Core-based English tests disregard grammar, spelling, mechanics, and usage," John Locke Foundation Spotlight Report, May 16, 2013, www.johnlocke.org/research/show/spotlights/287.

78. Erik Robelen, "NAEP Faces Budget Ax: Social Studies Exams To Be Scaled Back," *Curriculum Matters* (blog), *Education Week,* May 14, 2013, http://blogs.edweek.org/edweek /curriculum/2013/05/naep_faces_budget_ax_social_st.html.

79. Robin Lake and Tricia Maas, "Will Charter Schools Lead or Lag?" in *Common Core Meets Education Reform.*

80. Ibid., 80, 85.

CHAPTER 7

Holding Students to Account

Paul E. Peterson

The American high school is troubled. Not only do US high school students' performances trail those of students in most other industrialized nations, but there are few signs of improvement within the United States. While pupils in fourth grade have made striking gains over the past couple of decades, the gains attenuate by eighth grade and disappear altogether in high school. Even the most talented high school students don't always do well. Only 7 percent of US students score at or above the advanced level in mathematics, as compared to twice that percentage on the part of Canadians, Germans, Finns, Dutch, Belgians, and Japanese. Students in high-flying places such as Korea, Switzerland, and Singapore do even better.[1] Many students graduate from high school without the requisite skills needed to perform successfully in a modern, industrialized society. Approximately 1.7 million college students must take remedial courses, a clear indication that high school graduates have not acquired a minimum set of cognitive skills.

The causes are multiple, and no one fix will address them all. But flaws in the country's student accountability system are a likely contributing factor. Unlike most countries that have high-performing students, the United States lacks, as do most states within the United States, a set of exit exams, that is, subject-specific examinations students are expected to take as their careers in secondary schools are concluding. Other accountability mechanisms are weak as well. For example, the SAT, the test upon which selective colleges and universities rely heavily in their admission decisions, is disconnected from the high school curriculum. The governing board for the SAT frankly states that takers need no more than minimal preparation, adding to the sense that little needs to be done in high school to prepare for the future. The federally funded Pell grants, amounting to $36 billion annually, are provided to college students according to a formula based solely on student and family income, with no attention paid to the applicant's high school performance (beyond the acquisition of a high school diploma or its equivalent). Eligibility for participation in the federally guaranteed student loan program is also based on need, not merit.

Traditionally, teachers themselves were expected to hold students accountable. They graded students' tests and papers, and in elementary school they recommended pupils for promotion to the next grade level if their performance so warranted. High school students were graded strictly. Those who failed to achieve at the minimum acceptable level were asked to take the course a second time. Those who did well were given well-considered letters of recommendation for admission to colleges deemed appropriate. Those who did poorly adjusted to the situation by taking less demanding vocational courses or by withdrawing from high school altogether.

Teacher judgments were certainly affected by the social, cultural, and even political prejudices of the day. The English grammar school was notorious for its snobbery. Margaret Thatcher's biographer, Charles Moore, wrote that Dorothy Gillies, the headmistress of Kesteven and Grantham Girls' School, thought Thatcher "needed taking down a peg." No matter how talented the future prime minister may have been, she was, after all, only the daughter of a grocer. When Thatcher insisted on applying to Oxford at age seventeen, Miss Gillies declared: "I'm afraid you can't. You haven't got Latin." She refused to provide instruction in the subject. So Margaret took the subject from a Latin master at a boys' school and submitted a successful application to Oxford nonetheless. "Margaret never forgot what she considered to have been [the headmistress'] obstruction," her biographer continues. When Miss Gillies used a Latin phrase to welcome her to the podium as the main speaker at a major school event many years later, Thatcher corrected the Latin phrasing that had been used.[2] There is no evidence that Thatcher's self-esteem suffered unduly during her grammar school years. But she and her fellow students knew that much, if not quite everything, depended on the opinions of their grammar school teachers and principals.

Admittedly, the route to higher education has never been as tightly controlled in the United States as in England. But American variants of the Thatcher story are hardly unknown. Accordingly, progressive reformers dismantled many of the traditional accountability pillars in order to minimize the potential for social discrimination. Progressives also proposed that students be routinely promoted from one grade to the next regardless of their academic performance. It was widely thought that children's self-esteem would suffer if they did not keep pace with their peers. More recently, progressive reformers have asked high schools to minimize their dropout rates, as a high school diploma is regarded as critical to future success. Unfortunately, such pressures may encourage teachers to treat shoddy work as acceptable or, in the extreme but not unusual instance, ignore the fact that the student has done no work at all beyond regular occupation of a seat in the back of the room. Also in response to social pressure, high school grades have been inflated. Higher grades are given to maintain popularity with students and to give them a better chance of acceptance by a college or university. Even when students disturb the functioning of the school their rights can take precedence. The Supreme Court has given students a property right to an education that prevents suspension from school for ten days or more unless certain procedures—multiple witnesses, opportunities for cross-examination—are followed. Lower courts have ruled that student possessions may not be searched unless a legal justification is provided. Step by step, the authority of teachers and principals has become more ambiguous, undermining their capacity to hold students accountable.

Since traditional authority structures have broken down, new external accountability systems are needed today more than ever. In some states, elementary school students are being asked to perform at a minimum level in reading and math before being promoted to the next grade level. In other places, the transition from middle school to high school is determined by academic performance or by an external examination. In this paper, we focus on the exit exam, because it promises to be the antidote for the most dysfunctional institutional component of the American educational system: the high school. It is here where school authority is particularly problematic and student performance is especially mediocre, as indicated by student performance on the National Assessment of Educational Progress (NAEP). We also focus on the exit exam because the introduction of online learning systems into secondary education cannot be achieved without the establishment of an independently audited, subject-specific set of examinations that will hold these new educational vehicles accountable. When students and teachers are not in direct contact with one another, it is all the more important that a third party assesses whether learning has taken place. Indeed, the introduction of digital learning into secondary education, coupled with the establishment of the Common Core State Standards, provides a new opportunity to put into place a comprehensive, nationwide system of exit examinations that can provide guidance to employers as well as institutions of higher education.

When we recommend exit exams in this paper we mean by that phrase a system of independently audited, subject-specific, external examinations. Although the phrase is also used to identify minimum competency examinations that high school sophomores are expected to pass, our discussion of those policies should not be taken as an endorsement of them.

Exit Examinations and Student Motivation

In the absence of well-designed exit examinations, high school students and their teachers frequently find themselves at loggerheads. As long ago as 1965, University of Chicago sociologist James Coleman observed that high schools are "like jails, the military and factories; they are run by an 'administrative corps' that makes demands upon a larger group (students, prisoners, soldiers, workers)." In response, the larger group develops a set of norms that govern the choices individuals make: "The same process which occurs among prisoners in a jail and among workers in a factory are there, and the students develop a collective response to these demands," Coleman said. In all cases, the group pressure seeks to hold down effort to a level which can be maintained by all. "The students' name for the rate-buster is the 'curve-raiser' . . . and their methods of enforcing the work-restricting norms are similar to those of workers—ridicule, kidding, exclusion from the group."[3]

Cornell University economist John Bishop refers to such kidding and group exclusion as "nerd harassment," a particularly odious form of bullying because it discourages all students from full engagement with their studies.[4] For that reason Bishop advocates exit exams that relieve teachers of the responsibility for setting standards of performance and helps them identify objectives and motivate students toward clear goals. The teacher then becomes the coach who helps the student leap an external hurdle rather than the authority figure who stands in the way of achievement. Peer group relationships within a school become less competitive when students can help one another reach a common objective.

Without exit exams, students lack clear guidelines as to the material they are expected to learn or the level of proficiency they need to display. If the measure of performance is set by each individual teacher, students have an incentive to shop for "gut courses" offered by teachers who have low expectations and to bargain with each teacher for an acceptable grade.

Unless students are motivated to learn, education reform efforts are at risk. As Theodore Sizer, former dean of the Harvard Graduate School of Education, put it: "The student is the crucial actor. Whether we adults like it or not, he or she decides what has been purveyed." Unfortunately, he continued, "the American high school student, as *student*, is all too often docile, compliant, and without initiative."[5] Others have observed that American high schools have become shopping malls where students take courses as they please and students strike an implicit bargain with teachers: We won't expect much of you, if you don't expect much of us. Arthur G. Powell, Eleanor Farrar, and David K. Cohen describe this situation in *The Shopping Mall High School*:

> [Students] chose courses that were easy, met at convenient times, and enrolled their friends. They did homework, as long as it was not too much. . . . They never complained when little was expected of them. 'Why should we? We just want to get out.' They thought their teachers probably felt the same way. They were as much 'goof-offs' as the students. Avoidance treaties were mutually advantageous—they had found the like.[6]

Exit exams provide an opportunity to change the culture of the American high school. If students are expected to meet these standards, and if teachers are evaluated according to how well they bring students up to these standards, a new implicit bargain might emerge. Ideally, one might hear students say something like the following: "If you coach us in ways that will help us meet the standards that have been set, then we will focus our talent and energies on the task at hand." Cynics may find this to be a romantic notion. But as Al Shanker, the former head of the American Federation of Teachers, once pointed out, students must be held to a standard if teachers are to be evaluated on the basis of student performance. "Imagine we should shut down a hospital and fire its staff because not all of its patients became healthy," he argued, "but never demand that the patients also look out for themselves by eating properly, exercising, and laying off cigarettes."

Current Accountability Practice

There is no national exit exam policy in the United States set either by the federal government or by a consortium of state governments. US policy stands in contrast to the practice in many other countries. In England, for example, students at age 16 are expected to take "ordinary" or "O" level exams in several subjects. If they remain in secondary school beyond that age, they take "advanced" or "A" level exams. Similar policies are in place in France, Germany, Australia, and many other countries. Practice in Canada varies by province. In Alberta, student performance on an external examination determines 50 percent of the grade in relevant courses taken by graduating seniors. In many Asian countries (Japan, Korea, Singapore), performance on exit exams is the key to access to the university system. In all these instances, student performance is evaluated at multiple levels of accomplishment rather than on a simple, dichotomous pass/fail basis.

In 2011, twenty-four states asked students to pass a test in order to graduate from high school.[7] The movement began in Texas, when Ross Perot inaugurated a "pass to play" campaign that banned participation in sports and other extracurricular activities by those who did not earn a "C" in the classroom. Perhaps because of these origins, Southern and border states constitute thirteen of the twenty-three states that require exit exams. However, exams in most states do not require knowledge of specific subject matter taught in high school courses; instead, they are general math and reading exams for which no specific subject-matter knowledge is expected. Further, exam-passing thresholds are set at such low levels that the test constitutes a challenge only for the lowest-performing students.[8]

The state of New York does have subject-specific exit exams, which are known as Regents exams, named after the state board responsible for education policy. These exams were put in place during the Civil War when New York wanted to make sure that state-funded private schools were not admitting students willy-nilly so as to get state aid while helping young men avoid the draft. Today, to earn a Regents diploma, students must score sixty-five out of one hundred points on exams in English, global history and geography, US history and geography, a math subject, and a science subject. Bishop estimates that the exams have a positive impact on student performance in New York State,[9] but further studies are needed to identify their impact precisely.

Some have argued that Advanced Placement (AP) exams serve as the functional equivalent of a comprehensive system of subject-specific, externally validated exit exams. It is true that many (but certainly not all) high schools offer some AP courses that prepare students for one or more of the thirty-four end-of-course examinations available from Education Testing Service (ETS), a nationally respected, private testing agency. In recent years, about a third of all students who graduate from high school have enrolled in such a course. According to ETS, the number of students "passing" an AP exam in at least one subject (scoring at least a three on a five-point scale) increased from a little over three hundred thousand in 2002 to nearly five hundred and seventy-five thousand in 2012. But that number is still less than 20 percent of high school graduates and only about 15 percent of all those in the age cohort (as only about 75 percent of high school students graduate within four years). However, these numbers do not tell us the percentage of students who pass several examinations at level four or level five, which colleges typically use to decide whether student performance is high enough to allow advanced placement. Our best estimate, based on the number of passed tests and the average number of tests taken by any one student, is that only 7 percent to 8 percent of the age cohort in 2012 passed at a level necessary to secure an advanced placement in most institutions of higher education.[10] In other words, over 90 percent of those in recent age cohorts are not performing at a reasonably high level on any externally administered, subject-specific examination, a possible explanation for the much lower percentage of US students than students in many other advanced industrial societies who are performing at the "advanced" level on international tests.

Effects on Student Performance

Although studies of the impact of exit exams on student performance in other countries are scarce, one careful study suggests that student performance is higher in countries that require such examinations.[11] Much of the research on exit exams within the United States focuses on the consequences for those who fail to pass exit exams, with little attention given to the possible boost in achievement among the graduating cohort as a whole. Yet a few estimates of the impact of merit-based scholarship programs on student achievement have been undertaken. A quasi-experimental study of the impact of a merit-based college scholarship program found positive effects on high school student performance in Kalamazoo, Michigan, for example.[12]

The impact of the exit exam policy in Massachusetts is worth noting, especially since the proficiency threshold for passing the state test is one of the highest in the United States. When the state in 2003 required students to pass the proficiency bar on the high school examination offered to tenth graders, critics claimed many

FIGURE 1. Year Test Required for Graduation and Student Math Test Performance in Massachusetts, 1998–2012

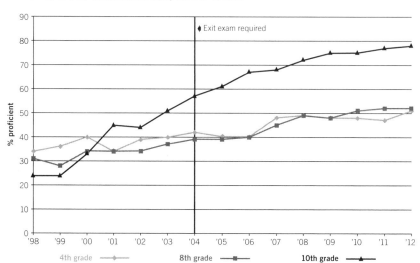

Note: To graduate from high school, a student must score at or above the proficiency level in tenth grade.

Source: Massachusetts Department of Education website: http://www.doe.mass.edu/mcas /2012/results/summary.pdf

students would fail. But when students were faced with the exam, the passing rate, even for first-time test-takers, shifted dramatically upward. Those who failed were given opportunities to take the test as many as five additional times. The number of students who never passed the exam was so small that the test quickly became an accepted practice. Significantly, student test performance climbed at other grade levels as well (fig. 1). The state's performance on NAEP also shifted upward so that it became the top-performing state in the country. Its performance on international tests ranks with the world's leaders. How much the introduction of a high school graduation examination requirement has contributed to recent gains in student performance in Massachusetts isn't known.[13] But the former secretary of education for the state of Massachusetts, David

Driscoll, during whose tenure the policy was introduced, attributes much of the state's success to the introduction of the exam requirement (even though he implemented numerous other policy changes as well).

These examples cannot be taken as anything other than suggestive evidence that exit exams have the desired consequences which Bishop and others anticipate. Much more scholarly work needs to be done to ascertain the long-term effects of exit examinations and merit-based college scholarships on student achievement and longer-term outcomes. Undoubtedly, much depends on the design of the policy.

Politics of Assessment

In principle, the American public is ready to support implementation of a more rigorous system of student accountability. According to the 2012 *Education Next* poll, 72 percent of Americans think that students should pass an exam before receiving a high school diploma, with only 12 percent opposed, the rest being indifferent. Also, 63 percent of the general public supports national standards, with another 30 percent indifferent, and only 7 percent standing in opposition. Levels of support for these policies are no less high among parents and teachers.

State political leaders may nonetheless be wary of setting more than minimal performance levels on exit exams. If too many students fail the exams, even after multiple attempts, state officers will be asked to lower the standards or explain low levels of student performance. Such pressures shaped the implementation of the federal law, No Child Left Behind.[14] Many states set low proficiency levels, thereby giving the appearance that more students were proficient in math and reading than was actually the case. Only five states—Massachusetts, Missouri, Washington, Hawaii, and New Mexico—set their state proficiency bar at the world-class level set by NAEP.[15] The low proficiency threshold set in California, for example, obscures the fact that it is among the ten states that have the lowest levels of student achievement.[16]

Not only have most states set a low proficiency bar, but pressures to ignore NCLB strictures intensified as the 2014 deadline drew nigh when the law expected all students to be proficient. As the deadline approached, increasing numbers of schools were found to have failed to meet expectations. Embarrassed by these developments, school districts attacked the NCLB standards, and the US Department of Education began providing state waivers that allowed many states to exempt themselves from NCLB requirements. One can expect similar political pressures to develop if exit exams are put into place.

Such political pressures might be addressed by establishing alternative examinations or by setting multiple cut points on one examination. Those students who wish to show high levels of competence (necessary for advanced placement in college or to boost their chances of winning admission to a selective college) could take the advanced version of the end-of-the-year examination, while other students could be given the opportunity to take the "ordinary" examination. In Great Britain, a similar arrangement expects all high school students to pass several "ordinary" examinations at age 16; those who want to demonstrate higher levels of competence are also examined later on at the "A" level in the subjects of their choice. Both exams have multiple cut points allowing for more precise evaluations of student performance than simple pass/fail. Similarly, the Regents examination in New York State can now be taken at either the "ordinary" or the "advanced" level.

New Opportunities Created by Online Learning

The need—and the likely demand—for external exams will accelerate as secondary schools enter the digital era and many more students take courses online. As in nineteenth-century New York when Regents exams were established, many competing providers are offering courses for credit in an environment where the temptation is to lower standards. Credit recovery courses—that is, courses repeated because the student withdrew from or failed the original course—are the fastest-growing segment of the online market today. In this segment, particularly, the downward pressure on course quality is intense. Uniform standards and proctored tests would allow for a public audit of these new instructional platforms and ensure that students take them seriously.

Separate from the spread of online learning courses is the current drive toward setting common standards and a common curriculum in core subjects across all the states. By these measures, advocates hope to boost student learning. But that can only happen if students are held accountable to a high proficiency level on the core curriculum, something that is best guaranteed by a system of external, proctored exit exams.

If students taking online courses are subject to external exams, the case for putting such exams into place more generally is greatly strengthened, especially given the current drive toward common standards. Yet the policy will not be adopted wholesale apart from a concerted political and policy effort. The political will cannot come, in the first instance, from elected officials or those campaigning for office. The groundwork for political action must be laid by serious study, high-quality research, informed commentary, and sustained articulation of concrete objectives. Unfortunately, research on the subject remains scattered. No major foundation has identified the policy as a matter of primary, or even secondary, importance. Only one small advocacy group, Washington, DC-based Achieve Inc., has consistently made the case for exit exams. As compared to the strenuous efforts that have been made on behalf of school accountability, merit pay, school vouchers, and charter schools, the case for exit exams has yet to be forcefully made by academic researchers, think-tank specialists, and policy advocates. Yet the public seems open to the idea, the potential benefits from its enactment seem large, and organized opposition to the policy has yet to be mobilized. With digital learning spreading into secondary education, the timing for action is particularly propitious.

Exam policies are set by states, not the federal government. But the federal government could accelerate the process by requiring that students seeking a Pell grant or a federally subsidized student loan pass an AP examination (or a comparable exit exam) in one or more courses.

Research Agenda

Given the state of the American high school, the most urgent topic begging for research attention is the high school exit exam. Currently, we do not have an objective compilation or system of classification of exit examination practices around the world or within the United States. In some countries the student elects to be examined in two or more specific subjects at either the ordinary or the advanced level, while in other places the test provides only a measure of mathematical and literacy proficiency. In some places, the test provides a rich set of information to those given access to the student's performance, while other exams are simply graded pass/fail. Exit exam systems vary in many other ways as well. A descriptive compilation and classification of the exit exam systems found throughout the industrialized world would be a valuable contribution useful to practitioners and researchers alike.

Experimental and quasi-experimental studies that estimate the impact of a wide variety of exit examination systems would enhance our understanding of the conditions under which they have the most positive effects. When examination systems are introduced, modified, or terminated, the change in policy often provides an opportunity to identify the specific impacts on students if outcome data are available both before and after the policy change is introduced. Once exit exams are placed on the policy agenda, the scholarly community can be expected to find ingenious methods for estimating policy impacts. What is needed now is a sense of urgency.

Notes

1. Eric A. Hanushek, Paul E. Peterson, and Ludger Woessmann, *Endangering Prosperity: A Global View of the American School* (Washington, DC: Brookings Institution Press, 2013).

2. Charles Moore, *Margaret Thatcher: From Grantham to the Falklands* (New York: Knopf, 2013), 37–39.

3. The quotations come from James S. Coleman, *The Adolescent Society: The Social Life of the Teen-ager and Its Impact on Education* (New York: The Free Press of Glencoe, 1961).

4. John H. Bishop, "Nerd Harassment, Incentives, School Priorities, and Learning," in *Earning and Learning: How Schools Matter,* ed. Susan Mayer and Paul E. Peterson (Washington, DC: Brookings Institution Press, 1999), 232–233.

5. Theodore Sizer, *Horace's Compromise* (New York: Houghton Mifflin, 1984), 54.

6. Arthur G. Powell, Eleanor Farrar, and David K. Cohen, *The Shopping Mall High School: Winners and Losers in the Educational Marketplace* (Boston: Houghton Mifflin, 1985), 19.

7. *Digest of Education Statistics,* 2011, National Center for Education Statistics, table 177.

8. Thomas Dee, "The 'First Wave' of Accountability," in *No Child Left Behind? The Politics and Practice of School Accountability,* ed. Paul E. Petersen and Martin R. West (Washington, DC: Brookings Institution Press, 2003).

9. Bishop, "Nerd Harassment."

10. Although ETS does not provide the exact numbers of students who scored at least a four on one exam in publicly available data, nearly 40 percent of the exams that receive a grade of three, four, or five are scored a three. To achieve our estimate we divided the number of tests passed at levels four and five by the average number of tests taken by a single student (three and

a half tests) and then divided that number by the number of seventeen-year-olds in the population in 2012. The 7 percent to 8 percent of the age cohort passing at the four and five level in 2012 is up from 3.5 percent in 2002.

11. Ludger Woessmann, "Central Exit Exams and Student Achievement: International Evidence," in *No Child Left Behind?*, ed. Peterson and West.

12. Timothy Bartik and Marta Lachowska, "The Short-Term Effects of the Kalamazoo Promise Scholarship on Student Outcomes" (working paper, Upjohn Institute, 2012).

13. Achieve, "Do Graduation Tests Measure Up? A Closer Look at State High School Exit Exams" (Washington, DC: Achieve Inc., 2004.)

14. NCLB asks schools to test all students in grades three through eight and once in high school. Districts were told to report aggregate student performance at each school, and each year schools were expected to make "adequate yearly progress" toward a goal of 100 percent student proficiency by the year 2014. Penalties were imposed upon schools that fell short of meeting the goals established by the law. But nothing in the law held students responsible for their own performance.

15. Paul E. Peterson and Peter Kaplan, "Despite Common Core, States Still Lack Common Standards," *Education Next* 13, no. 4 (Fall 2013); and Paul E. Peterson and Carlos X. Lastra-Anadón, "State Standards Rise in Reading, Fall in Math," *Education Next* 10, no. 4 (Fall 2010): 12–16.

16. Hanushek, Peterson, and Woessmann, *Endangering Prosperity*.

Part III: *Resources and Research*

CHAPTER 8

Strengthening the Curriculum

Tom Loveless

In the nineteenth century, Herbert Spencer famously posed the question underlying all curricula: what knowledge is of most worth? Conflicting answers to that question have generated political controversy throughout the history of the American school—and especially in the 1990s—primarily because of a philosophical conflict between what have become known as traditionalist and progressive camps. This essay sketches the evolution of that conflict from the 1990s to the current day and evaluates its impact on the content and breadth (time spent on subjects) of the school curriculum. Although the most heated curriculum wars quieted down by the mid-2000s, two forces loom on the horizon that may reignite them: new technologies and the Common Core State Standards. Indeed, skirmishes over the Common Core have already taken place. I conclude by discussing specific areas in which future research can make meaningful contributions.

The 1990s Curriculum Wars

The 1990s featured fierce battles over curriculum in the four major K–12 school subjects: reading, math, science, and history. In reading, believers in "whole language" methods struggled with phonics and code-based advocates. In math, the NCTM (National Council of Teachers of Mathematics) standards documents first swept unopposed across the land—spawning new textbooks and dominating policies ranging from National Assessment of Educational Progress tests to National Science Foundation grants to state standards and assessments before confronting a powerful backlash. In science, advocates of hands-on, project-based learning struggled with advocates of content-oriented curriculum. And in history, multiculturalists and believers that the teaching of US history should devote more time to past national sins (in particular, the mistreatment of blacks, Hispanics, Asians, Native Americans, and women) struggled with opponents who charged them with foisting an ideological agenda on the schools.

The curriculum wars were fueled by the rise of standards in the late 1980s and early 1990s. Progressives and traditionalists had argued over the curriculum throughout the twentieth century. But the arguments had mostly remained confined to education schools, perhaps bubbling up in communities that adopted new textbooks or curriculum guidelines.[1] Primarily, this was an argument among academic rivals and professional educators. That all changed when standards and assessments were pinned to accountability systems. The notion that states declare the learning objectives schools should pursue, and perhaps even attach rewards or sanctions to their attainment, ratcheted up the importance of the official curriculum adopted by authorities.

The curriculum wars then subsided. What happened? Science and history debates were pushed aside, at least from the public stage, by the focus on reading and math in state and federal education reform. "Whole language" was routed from state-level reading policy by more than one hundred bills passed by legislatures.[2] The 1998 federal Reading Excellence Act supported programs backed by "scientifically based reading research," a mandate reiterated in Reading First, a component of the No Child Left Behind Act in 2002. Some of the tenets of whole language—workshop models of instruction, an emphasis on student-centered learning, the prominence of authentic texts—were absorbed into (and some would say disguised by) "balanced literacy" reading programs.

In mathematics, the NCTM moved back toward the middle of the progressive-traditionalist continuum, first with a more moderate set of standards in 2000 and then, dramatically, with the release of "Curriculum Focal Points" in 2006. The treatment of whole number arithmetic illustrates the philosophical shift. The 1989 standards urged teachers to de-emphasize computation skills in favor of problem-solving, going so far as to disparage the elementary grades' teaching of whole numbers and fractions as outmoded "shopkeeper arithmetic." Calculators could take care of any future computational needs. "Focal Points" not only endorsed the learning of whole numbers and fractions, it made them the centerpiece of the elementary math curriculum. As the country moved into a new century, the most controversial of the 1990s math reform curricula lost market share and vanished. Publication of *MathLand*, at one time the most widely used textbook series in California, was halted in 2007.

Time on Subjects

An empirical means of tracking changes in curricular emphasis is to examine the amount of time schools spend on the core subjects. Tests mandated by NCLB and state accountability systems compelled schools to focus on reading and math and on the attainment of basic skills by low-achieving students. Critics charged that such an emphasis narrowed the curriculum. There is evidence supporting the charge but conflicting accounts on the magnitude of the narrowing. From 1988 to 2004, the Schools and Staffing Survey teacher questionnaires indicated that teachers in grades one through four increased time spent teaching English language arts and math by about an hour per week, with a commensurate decrease in social science and science.[3] A 2004 study in Florida found that schools labeled as failing on the Florida Comprehensive Assessment Test (FCAT) spent an inordinate amount of time in the following year teaching writing, the section of the FCAT that the state's educators believed was most amenable to improvement.[4] A pre-NCLB study of Kentucky classrooms by the Rand Corporation exploited the fact that accountability in that state was linked to different subjects in different grades.[5] It found that fourth-grade teachers spent about four hours more per week on the subjects targeted for improvement in fourth grade, while fifth-grade teachers spent about six more hours a week on the subjects tested in fifth grade.

The Center on Education Policy surveyed district superintendents in 2007 and asked them to estimate changes in instructional time from 2002–2007.[6] More than half (58 percent) reported that classroom teachers had increased the amount of time spent on English language arts; 45 percent reported increased time on math instruction. Districts that increased time on English language arts averaged an additional 141 minutes per week on the subject; for math, the figure was 89 minutes. A significant percentage of districts reported decreased time spent on social studies (36 percent), science (28 percent), and art/music (16 percent).

In sum, over the past fifteen years the content of the curriculum has been buffeted by longstanding philosophical debates. In the 1990s, math and reading were both strongly controlled by progressive ideas, but that influence was subsequently diminished by federal and state legislative action and the rise of accountability systems focused on basic skills. Arguments over science and social studies/history were pushed out of the limelight. Accountability systems have also precipitated a shift in instructional time away from non-tested subjects in favor of reading and mathematics. To critics, narrowing the curriculum is bad, but it has not generated much public opposition. To many people, narrowing the curriculum is nothing more than focusing on the essential knowledge and skills that all children must learn.

Compared to the 1990s, a relative calm presides over today's curriculum politics. What's in store for the future? Two powerful changes lie ahead that have the potential to provoke controversy by inflaming the old progressive-traditionalist philosophical debates.

New Technologies

The proliferation of computer-based instruction and online schooling has many observers excited by the promise of technology to fundamentally reshape education. Terry Moe and John Chubb[7] argue that once students are no longer dependent on brick-and-mortar schooling, the mammoth institutions built to deliver traditional instruction—and the entrenched interest groups (e.g., unions) that benefit from current institutional arrangements—will wither away. Clayton M. Christensen, Michael B. Horn, and Curtis W. Johnson argue in *Disrupting Class: How Disruptive Innovation Will Change the Way the World Learns* that technology will "change how the world learns."[8] They foresee a digital storehouse of modular online learning activities that can be customized to each student. Although technology may indeed change how students learn, the curricular question is whether it will also change *what* students learn.

The Christensen book answers that question by invoking a romantic ideology with deep roots in educational progressivism. The theories of modern-day progressives are called on to endorse curricula based on students' interests and strengths.[9] Howard Gardner's theory of multiple intelligences asserts that conventional schooling only taps two intelligences (linguistic and logical-mathematical) and ignores six others. Christensen et al. embrace Gardner's ideas and argue that curricula customized to students' intelligences will enhance learning, mainly by boosting students' motivation to learn. E. D. Hirsch points out in *The Schools We Need: And Why We Don't Have Them* that Gardner's theory lacks empirical evidence and has few followers among cognitive psychologists; despite that, it appeals to those with "the benign hope for all children that they will be good at doing something and happy doing it."[10]

Christensen, Horn, and Johnson also embrace a close cousin of multiple intelligences: learning styles theory, the notion that students learn material best that is presented "in ways that correspond to how their minds are wired to learn." The authors call for new assessments that will accommodate different learning styles, describing a student who, "blessed with bodily-kinesthetic intelligence" but weak in mathematics, struggles to learn chemistry: "we'll need to find ways to compare his mastery of a body of material with the mastery demonstrated by someone whose intelligence is in the logical-mathematical realm."[11] This sounds an awful lot like a chemistry test for athletes and dancers.

Daniel T. Willingham has debunked learning styles. Writing in the *Washington Post,* Willingham explains:

> The Big Idea behind learning styles is that kids vary in how they learn: Some learn best by looking (visual learners), some by listening (auditory learners), and some by manipulating things (kinesthetic learners).
>
> The prediction is straightforward: Kids learn better when they are taught in a way that matches their learning style than when they are taught in a way that doesn't.
>
> That's a straightforward prediction.
>
> The data are straightforward too: It doesn't work.[12]

The point here is that the proliferation of new technologies will not only affect instruction, the *how* of learning, but may also affect curriculum, the *what* of learning. That proposition is sure to ignite the historical conflict between educational progressives and traditionalists. Moreover, individualized instructional programs, whether delivered exclusively online or through "blended" regimes, are antithetical to the goal that all students learn a common body of knowledge and skills at approximately the same time.

If individual interests and pre-existing cognitive skills determine what is learned and when it is learned (i.e., "each student learns at her own pace"), demographic characteristics that are correlated with personal interests and cognitive skills will mirror how far students proceed through the curriculum. Achievement gaps based on socioeconomic characteristics will surely widen and solidify.

Common Core

The Common Core State Standards project starts from a premise diametrically opposed to the technologists' philosophy of individualism. Common Core supporters believe the content of learning should reflect what a society wants students to learn, that such content can be spelled out with specificity, and that assessments should measure whether students have learned, and schools have taught, the authorized content by a stipulated time. A math standard stating that by the end of second-grade students will know how to subtract one three-digit number from another three-digit number does not mean students will learn it at their own pace, with some mastering the idea in second grade and others taking two or three more years to learn it. Nor does it mean students will learn subtraction when they find it interesting or only after they have grown tired of drawing unicorns.

The description just presented casts the Common Core in terms appealing to education traditionalists. But many traditionalists are critical of the Common Core. Why? Because the Common Core also contains elements that are currently ambiguous as to the ends they are intended to accomplish. These elements are fuel for rekindling the progressive-traditionalist curriculum wars.

Keep an eye on these flashpoints:

1. Process over product. The Common Core can be used to justify many things, including questionable approaches to learning. When a particular activity comes under fire, local educators

seek political cover by claiming that district or state policies (or the Common Core) made them do it. Recently, the Common Core project released "Standards for Mathematical Practice," guidelines related to practice, not content.[13] Giving process equal status with content drew the ire of traditionalists in the 1990s math wars.

Consider the following anecdote. James V. Shuls, a blogger on education topics, pulled his son, a first grader, out of the local public school because of its interpretation of practice commensurate with the Common Core.[14] The school used a constructivist math textbook, *Cognitively Guided Instruction,* that was written during the heyday of the 1989 NCTM Standards. The book is now making a comeback as "aligned with the Common Core."

Students in the class were forbidden to add numbers in a column. Instead, they were forced to decompose the numbers and show them graphically (draw them), as called for in the Common Core. The parents met with the teacher and principal. The teacher claimed this laborious approach (based on math theories from the Freudenthal Institute, also the founders of the Programme for International Student Assessment, or PISA test) revealed students' conceptual understanding of addition, an example of the "deeper learning" called for in the Common Core. The school's principal also defended the approach for reflecting the objectives of the Common Core.

2. Non-fiction texts. English language arts teachers are up in arms over the Common Core's suggestion that teachers should try to balance the assignment of non-fiction and fiction readings. This criticism is mostly inside baseball, limited to English Language Arts (ELA) teachers. Common Core leaves the selection of texts to local educators. The real battles will come when stories surface of teachers assigning controversial texts as required readings. Controversial texts are assigned currently, of course. But in the future, the Common Core will be cited as justification (again, providing political cover).

3. Integrated math courses. Math reformers have long dreamed of eliminating year-long high school math courses taught by topic (algebra, geometry, calculus) in favor of integrated math courses that weave major topics together in composite courses called math I, math II, math III (equivalent to freshman math, sophomore math, junior math, etc.). Most of the world's countries currently organize math curriculum in the integrated way; the United States is an outlier in not doing so. But this reform has been tried repeatedly (most recently in the state of Georgia) and it has repeatedly failed after stern public opposition. Many teachers are not comfortable teaching an integrated math course, and parents fear taking such a course will jeopardize their children's preparation for college. Currently only 3–4 percent of US high school students in any particular grade (and less than 10 percent of all graduates) take an integrated math course. And yet, the Common Core accords integrated math and topic-oriented math courses equal standing, with standards and assessments written for both. This is understood to be a way of encouraging the use of integrated math courses. Seattle schools have already announced their intention to switch to integrated courses. Watch for a firestorm of opposition in many communities.

4. Tracking. William Schmidt of the University of Chicago has declared that the Common Core means an end to tracking in math through eighth grade. Tracking typically starts in seventh or eighth grade, placing kids in courses that match the hierarchy of the math curriculum. Nationally, about 6 percent of seventh graders take algebra I. Students who take and pass algebra I typically then take geometry or algebra II in eighth grade because, presumably, they are prepared for it. That would end. De-tracking created political turmoil in many communities in the 1990s. Look for controversy to return if the Common Core is interpreted as meaning all students will take the exact same courses.

Future Research

The phenomena described in this essay are political in nature. They stem from ancient philosophical disagreements over what students should learn. Progressives and traditionalists battled over the curriculum in the first two decades of the twentieth century (practical vs. "book-based" learning), in the 1920s (project-based, experiential learning vs. traditional intellectual disciplines), in the 1940s (curriculum for personal adjustment vs. curriculum for knowledge and skills), in the 1960s and 1970s (student-centered, open classrooms and inquiry learning vs. teacher-led classrooms and basic skills), and in the 1990s (over standards, as described above). It is reasonable to believe that the politics of curriculum, which have been relatively dormant in the past decade, will become heated once again.

Two catalysts for igniting curricular controversies have been identified: technology and the Common Core. The controversies that lie on the horizon offer opportunities for important research. Here are four ideas:

First, much more research is needed on the effectiveness of different curricula. We need to find out what works, whether it is progressive or traditional in approach. The trick is to identify a set of outcomes that rival camps believe are worthy of attainment. Mathematica managed to do this with a randomized controlled trial of four elementary math curricula, but that kind of study is rare.

Second, research is needed on the impact of the Common Core on curriculum as the implementation of standards and tests unfolds. Will students really be taught knowledge and skills that were not taught in the past? Are all of those programs advertised as "Common Core compatible" truly different from previous programs?

Third, the linkages between curriculum and instruction are not well-researched. A common refrain of advocates is that teachers will have to teach differently to realize the potential of the

Common Core. OK, that's interesting but vague. Empirical evidence is needed showing that a particular set of instructional strategies is optimal when paired with a particular set of curricular objectives.

Fourth, the evidence on technology and learning is sparse. Good evaluations of online learning are needed, whether curricula are flipped or blended or totally digital. Opponents are currently having a field day criticizing the low test scores of virtual charter schools.

Notes

1. The most famous incident took place in 1974 in Kanawha County, West Virginia. Objections to a new language arts curriculum led to school boycotts, shotgun attacks on school buses, a school bombing, and a statewide miners' strike. See "The Great Textbook War," American Radio Works, http://americanradioworks.publicradio.org/features/textbooks/books_and_beliefs.html.

2. Richard L. Allington, "Does Federal and State Reading Policymaking Matter?" in *The Great Curriculum Debate: How Should We Teach Reading and Math?*, ed. Tom Loveless (Washington, DC: Brookings Institution Press, 2002), 268–298.

3. Beth A. Morton and Ben Dalton, "Changes in Instructional Hours in Four Subjects by Public School Teachers of Grades 1 Through 4," National Center for Education Statistics, 2007.

4. Dan Goldhaber and Jane Hannaway, "Accountability with a Kicker: Preliminary Observations on the Florida A+ Accountability Plan," *Phi Delta Kappan* 85, no. 8 (2004), 598–605. (Reprinted in *Annual Editions: Education 05/06, 32nd Edition*, ed. Fred Schultz [Dubuque, Iowa: McGraw-Hill/Dushkin, 2005], 69–75.)

5. Brian M. Stecher and Sheila I. Barron, "Quadrennial Milepost: Accountability Testing in Kentucky," National Center for Research on Evaluation, Standards and Student Testing

(CRESST)/Rand Education (Los Angeles: University of California, June 1999), 15–17.

6. Jennifer McMurrer, "Choices, Changes, and Challenges: Curriculum and Instruction in the NCLB Era," Center on Education Policy, July 24, 2007, http://www.cep-dc.org /displayDocument.cfm?DocumentID=312.

7. Terry M. Moe and John E. Chubb, *Liberating Learning: Technology, Politics, and the Future of American Education* (San Francisco: Jossey-Bass, 2009).

8. Clayton M. Christensen, Michael B. Horn, and Curtis W. Johnson, *Disrupting Class: How Disruptive Innovation Will Change the Way the World Learns* (New York: McGraw-Hill, 2008).

9. In addition to Howard Gardner, the book favorably cites Tony Wagner, author of *The Global Achievement Gap: Why Even Our Best Schools Don't Teach the New Survival Skills Our Children Need—and What We Can Do About It* (New York: Basic Books, 2008) and Larry Rosenstock, principal of technology-oriented, inquiry- and project-based High Tech High in San Diego. Rosenstock says that High Tech High grew out of his work with Ted Sizer, a progressive legend, former dean of Harvard Graduate School of Education, and founder of the Coalition of Essential Schools.

10. E. D. Hirsch Jr., *The Schools We Need: And Why We Don't Have Them* (New York: Doubleday, 1996), 261.

11. Christensen, Horn, and Johnson, *Disrupting Class*, 112.

12. Daniel Willingham, "Student Learning Styles Theory is Bunk," *Washington Post*, September 14, 2009.

13. Common Core State Standards Initiative, "Standards for Mathematical Practice," 2012, http://www.corestandards.org /Math/Practice.

14. James Shuls, "Why We Need School Choice," *Education News*, January 16, 2013, http://www.educationnews.org/education -policy-and-politics/james-shuls-why-we-need-school-choice.

CHAPTER 9

Covering the Costs

Caroline M. Hoxby

Most Americans, whether employers or parents or people who do business internationally, recognize that our students' achievement is mismatched with our economy. The growing sectors of our economy are highly skill-intensive, and only the shrinking sectors require unskilled laborers. Yet, as evinced by scores on the National Assessment of Educational Progress (NAEP), the share of our population that is capable of performing highly skilled jobs is no greater than it was forty years ago. Our students' achievement is mediocre compared to the achievement of the people worldwide with whom they will have to compete for jobs in the future. For instance, American fifteen-year-olds scored below the average in mathematics in 2009 among students in member nations of the Organisation for Economic Co-operation and Development (OECD). They merely scored at the average in reading.[1] Moreover, in the future, US students will not compete only with OECD students. They will compete with millions of people from countries like India and China where the number of well-educated young adults is growing very rapidly.

The recognition that American students must improve is not enough, however. The United States needs to find the methods and the resources to make the improvements. In this paper, I examine some of the methods that hold the greatest promise and argue that they are affordable with the resources we *already* have.

If the past few decades are anything to go by, we might scoff at the idea of improving American students' skills at no additional cost. From 1970 to 2010, per-pupil expenditure on public elementary and secondary education rose by 327 percent in dollars adjusted for inflation.[2] Over the same period, high school students' scores on the NAEP rose not at all. In reading, they scored 285.2 in 1971 and 296 in 2008. In mathematics, they scored 304 in 1973 and 306 in 2008.[3] In other words, achievement stubbornly failed to improve even when we "improved" schools in ways that required enormous increases in resources. Why, then, should we think that we might now be able to raise achievement without additional resources?

The answer is that, now, we are contemplating very different methods of improving schools. These methods are not only much more promising than the "improvements" conducted in the past. They are also more likely to pay for themselves because they move money toward the people who, and schools that, actually raise achievement and—crucially—move it *away* from those that do not. Put another way, these new methods tend to *align* resources with effectiveness, much as private markets do. Because these methods push schools into greater alignment with the private sector, the realignments are not only feasible but sustainable over the long term. This makes them differ fundamentally from previous "improvements" that required across-the-board increases in spending or that required omniscient regulators who somehow command-and-control in opposition to market forces.

Before we get to the new methods that can potentially pay for themselves, however, one might ask why containing cost growth in K–12 education is more important now than in the past. First and most important, skills are the crucial input for our growth industries. If the United States can only produce skills at much greater expense than other countries can, it will lose its comparative advantage in high-skill industries. Jobs in those industries will drain away to other countries with lower costs of producing skills. This is basic economics, and it matters much more than in decades past when few other countries produced educated people. Second, many Americans are disillusioned and exhausted by calls for further increases in education spending. They refuse to keep "throwing money at the problem." Third, for the last forty years, US schools have not been accurately reporting the true growth in their education spending. They have promised increasingly generous pensions to teachers and other staff members and put insufficient money into the trust funds intended to pay those pensions. The pensions are now due and will continue to be paid for decades. As a result, *even if spending on current students does not rise at all,* spending on public education will rise substantially simply to meet pension obligations to retired staff. Finally, rising health care costs have been crowding out education spending in government budgets for more than twenty years. They will continue to do so because of the aging of the population—even if health care inflation abates. All in all, it would be foolhardy to suggest that we improve US education via methods that require further, substantial increases in spending.

What are these new methods of improving American education that are both more promising than past methods and that can plausibly pay for themselves? They are:

   i. school choice and competition,

ii. rewarding teachers based on their value-added, and

iii. using technology to substitute for routine instruction and to customize instruction

What This Paper Is and Is Not About

It is the goal of this paper to outline what is *feasible* given the resources we have and what we know about methods of raising achievement. My goal is to describe financial models whereby schools could realize improvements without needing additional resources. In that sense, it is a realistic paper.

However, it is not the goal of this paper to predict or be constrained by the bastardized policies that fallible politicians often enact when they bow to pressures from lobbyists, public sector unions, fundraisers, and other interest groups. Politicians often misuse resources to pay for support, bribe opponents to be silent, or "grandfather" ineffective programs. They create programs with elements that undermine the intended policy—sometimes through mere incompetence, other times because some interest group prefers that the program self-destruct. While papers on the politics of education and the misuses of government funds are important for understanding the forces opposed to true reform, relentless attention to such topics obscures the possibilities for raising American students' skills.

Furthermore, this paper does not attempt a comprehensive review of the evidence on the effectiveness of the three improvement methods listed above. Nor does this paper attempt to "get into the weeds" of policies such as exactly how value-added can best be estimated. There are many papers that cover such topics.

Rather, the focus is novel: do logic and the available evidence suggest that new, promising methods of improving achievement can be implemented within current education budgets? The phrase "available evidence" is important. This paper does not purport to offer definitive evidence. Indeed, one of the goals of this paper is to suggest what evidence we need to gather via future policy experiments and future research.

Rewarding and Employing Teachers Based on Their Value-Added

In recent years, researchers have demonstrated that individual teachers differ substantially in their value-added—their propensity to raise students' achievement. For our purposes, the key takeaways from the research are as follows:

1. A teacher who is in the top 10 percent of the current distribution of value-added raises student achievement by several times what a teacher in the bottom 10 percent does.[4]

2. If all US teachers had value-added equal to what the current top 10 percent has, the average American student would achieve at the level of students whose parents have incomes in the top 10 percent of the family income distribution. This is approximately equivalent to the level at which the average student in Singapore achieves.[5]

3. Even after a single year of teaching, we can predict a teacher's value-added sufficiently well that the retention decision can be made at that point. Two years of teaching experience adds information, but subsequent years of teaching add little to our predictions.[6]

4. After the first few years of teaching (during which most teachers' value-added rises, apparently through on-the-job learning), a teacher's value-added remains fairly stable.[7]

5. Teachers' measured value-added based on students' test scores is highly correlated with their measured value-added based on long-term outcomes such as students' earnings, employment, and college attainment.[8]

6. Teachers' value-added on students' non-cognitive outcomes, such as truancy, attendance, and disciplinary incidents, can be measured and gives therefore a better fix on how teachers affect long-term outcomes.[9]

7. Teachers with master's degrees do not have systemically higher value-added. If anything, the evidence suggests that master's degrees are associated with lower value-added.[10]

8. There are almost no credentials that predict a teacher's value-added, with the exception that individuals who attended a more selective college tend to have higher value-added. This is presumably due not only to their higher aptitude and better education but also to the fact that selective colleges admit students in a fairly holistic way that rewards leadership, motivation, and similar traits.[11]

9. There is evidence that teachers improve their value-added when exposed to other teachers who have high value-added and when they are offered pay based on their value-added.[12]

Suppose that we wanted to have a pay system that attained the goal that all teachers (except the brand new, untried ones) would have value-added in the range we currently see among the top 10 percent of teachers (hereafter: "high value-added teachers"). A well-designed pay system would achieve this both through selection (getting the right individuals to become and stay teachers) and through incentives (giving teachers incentives to raise their value-added). What would such a system look like? First, within teaching, pay would be aligned with value-added. This would provide the right incentives for improvement. Second, to ensure that high value-added individuals select into teaching, their pay would have to be competitive with alternative jobs that they could obtain. Since the evidence suggests that people who can be high value-added teachers are also better at other jobs, we should assume that their alternative jobs will be those that a baccalaureate degree holder with above-average aptitude, college quality, and motivation could obtain. Note that these are *not* the alternative jobs that most current teachers now take if they leave teaching. This is because most current teachers have aptitude and college quality well below average among baccalaureate degree holders.

Consider some private sector occupations that are filled by people with baccalaureate or more education (but not a professional degree or PhD): accountants, compensation and benefits managers, computer programmers, editors, landscape architects and surveyors, property managers, occupational therapists, regional planners, public relations specialists, and buyers for major retail stores. These people are all paid based on their productivity and rewarded by private sector employers for their intelligence, motivation, and ability to work with other people. Benjamin Scafidi, David Sjoquist, and Todd Stinebrickner show that only about 5 percent of people who leave teaching ultimately take a job along these lines.[13] Sara Champion, Annalisa Mastri, and Kathryn Shaw show that the teachers who leave for such jobs are those whose value-added in teaching is unusually high.[14]

Let us say, then, that any high value-added teacher's compensation—pay plus benefits—must be equal to the average for full-time workers in these occupations.[15] Their average annual compensation was $89,989 in the 2009–10 school year (the most recent year for which full financial data on US schools are available).[16] Suppose that, by employing value-added-based pay and creating the right selection and incentives, US schools were able to attain a teaching workforce almost entirely composed of high value-added teachers. Would they have sufficient money to pay compensation of $89,989 to all teachers except untried, new ones? The answer is "yes" with current budgets. In the 2009–10 school year, public schools paid $275.3 billion in compensation (wages, salaries, payments for benefits) to instructors and employed 3,123,957 full-time equivalent classroom teachers.[17] This is $88,132 per teacher—enough to pay 95 percent of teachers the competitive compensation of $89,989 and pay the remaining 5 percent of teachers (presumably the untried ones) compensation of about $53,000. If, by employing only high value-added teachers, schools could eliminate instructional support staff (people who are not certified instructors but who help with instructional improvement, curriculum development, staff training, and the like), the average teacher might be paid $94,177 out of current budgets.[18]

Keep in mind that no adjustment has been made for the fact that teachers' contract hours are only about 1,200 hours per year (about 0.6 of full-time) and that teaching jobs have work hours, work locations, and vacation timing that allow them to avoid child care costs that the typical full-time worker must bear. Thus, it is generous to assume that they need to be compensated like someone who works full time. I have made such generous assumptions because *high* value-added teachers may actually work a good many more hours than their contract hours.

One might wonder how it is possible that US public schools could, within their current budgets, pay teachers in a manner that is so competitive with private sector rewards. The main explanation is that although high value-added teachers are currently underpaid, low value-added teachers who have high seniority, master's degrees, and other paper credentials are systemically overpaid relative to their alternative jobs. They have no incentive to leave teaching, therefore. They also have no incentive to improve their value-added. Low value-added teachers absorb so much of the total compensation budget that little is left for high value-added starting teachers, who are not only underpaid if they do teach but who tend to leave teaching as a result. A second, less important explanation is that a non-trivial share of instructional compensation goes to people who are not classroom teachers but who provide some form of instructional "assistance." Randomized controlled trials suggest that such assistants add little or no value in terms of student achievement.[19] As a logical matter, this may be because principals often steer incompetent teachers into non-classroom instructional jobs. That is, such jobs act as "holding tanks" for ineffective teachers who have not been dismissed—sometimes because of formal barriers to dismissal but more often because there is no norm of dismissal for mere incompetence.

Importantly, a system in which teachers are compensated in a manner that is fully competitive with their private sector alternatives would be highly sustainable. This is a major but often underappreciated benefit of education reforms that move schools in the direction of managing themselves as private organizations do. This is in contrast to well-meaning but starry-eyed educational methods that depend on school personnel being so altruistic or specially attuned to teaching that they are rare or ignore the fact that they are undercompensated.

Employing Technology to Enrich Instruction and Substitute for Mundane Instruction

The combination of modern computing, software, and the Internet has led various researchers and commentators to suggest that technology could substantially improve American education. The evidence on this front is still very slight, owing mainly to the absence of evidence from randomized controlled trials or similarly robust policy experiments.[20] However, there is fairly compelling logic to the claim. The logic is that current technology allows students to interact with course materials in a highly individuated way (as opposed to a non-individuated textbook, say), to obtain instant feedback and diagnosis in some subject areas (for instance, on mathematics problems), and to gain access to a rich array of auxiliary information via hyperlinks. Technology should also allow teachers and administrators to track students' progress—on some types of assessments, at least—fairly easily.

Suppose that we accept the idea that modern technology can enhance instruction and improve achievement. We must still grapple with the question of whether it can pay for itself. We ought not to be overly sanguine because previous waves of technology—television, instructional films, telephony, audio-visual machines, photocopying, central computers, and computers on teachers' desktops—appear simply to have added to schools' costs. When they were introduced, it was often argued that they would substitute for mundane instructional or logistical tasks and thus pay for themselves via reductions in school staff. It is nearly impossible to find evidence of this, given the unrelenting increase in the ratio of school staff to pupils over the years in which such technology was introduced.

What makes current technology more likely to generate cost savings than, say, television or instructional films? The key distinction is the degree of interactivity—which boils down to the claim that students can be "hooked" by software that responds to them in a way that they cannot be "hooked" by technology that allows them to be passive. Thus, the technology can keep them productive and engaged for non-trivial periods of time—periods that staff can allocate to other students and other tasks. Indeed, since almost no one claims that technology can substitute for some instructional tasks—motivating children, organizing projects, teaching higher level writing skills, diagnosing learning problems in a manner that requires empathy—the logic of modern technology is that staff should focus on the non-substitutable activities. They can then be spread more thinly among students because each student only needs to engage in non-substitutable activities for part of each day. This is known as the hybrid model—that is, a school in which students work with teachers part of the time and work on individual computers the remaining time.

As a logical matter, a hybrid school could improve achievement within current educational budgets. It just has to be the case that the necessary and substantial investments in technology (computers, networking, software, technology maintenance staff) are offset by reductions in other staff costs. This seems possible, but can it occur in practice?

Unfortunately, there is a paucity of hybrid schools in the United States owing to the newness of the hybrid model.[21] Since it is impossible to describe a large, representative sample of the hybrid schools that will probably exist in the future (since they do not exist now), it makes sense to take a case study approach and analyze one network of schools on which detailed, accurate financial information is available: the Rocketship schools located in Santa Clara County, California.

The Rocketship schools are hybrid schools that serve students who are largely poor and Hispanic or black. They attain some of the highest scores for students from such backgrounds among California schools.[22] Their students spend part of each day in a "learning lab" in which they work on computers. The schools also use computer-based technology for curricular enrichment, diagnosis, and tracking progress. (Although the Rocketship schools are charter schools and largely admit students via lottery, they have not yet been evaluated using lottery-based methods. Thus, some of their high performance may be due to motivated or able students' self-selecting into them. However, what really interests us here is their financial model.)

The Rocketship schools have current per-pupil expenditures equal to 79 percent of that of traditional public schools in their county: $7,492 for Rocketship and $9,463 per school year for the other schools.[23] How do they manage this? First, their ratio of pupils to classroom teachers is 30.5 while the traditional public schools' is 21.6. Thus, Rocketship schools need only two teachers for every three teachers whom the traditional public schools need. According to their accounts, this entire reduction is attained by means of computers being used for mundane instruction and practice of skills. Second, Rocketship schools spend a much lower share of their budget on the wages and salaries of *non*-teachers: 12.7 percent as opposed to 32.6 percent. This is largely because they have approximately one non-teaching staff member for every three such people at traditional public schools. The schools' explanation is that they have less need for administrators and support staff because technology performs many of the tracking and paperwork tasks that such people perform in traditional public schools.[24]

So far we have compared Rocketship to the traditional public schools only on the basis of current expenditures which include some spending for technology (software licenses, network access, staff for maintaining technology, and the like) but which do not include spending on computer hardware. However, in Santa Clara County, total capital outlay expenditure was $1,322 per pupil in the 2009–10 school year. It is simply not plausible that Rocketship spent a similar amount on capital that it would need regardless of whether it adopted a hybrid model (that is, the same sort of buildings and equipment that the traditional public schools have) and *then* spent an additional $1,971 per pupil on just the equipment needed for its hybrid model. With that additional expenditure, Rocketship could purchase two computers and associated networking equipment for every student every year. (In fact, if it did do this, it would be unable to count the computers as capital expenditures because capital must have a working life of more than a year.)

In other words, it is clear that Rocketship is able to use a hybrid model of instruction while staying well within the total per-pupil budget of local, traditional public schools.

The hybrid model is probably not the only reason why Rocketship schools have lower per-pupil current expenditure. They are charter schools so they have stronger incentives to use their funds efficiently than traditional public schools. They also have greater management autonomy than most traditional public schools.[25] These are points that I take up in the next section. However, the Rocketship financial model is a proof-of-concept. That is, it is proof that it is possible to reduce staff sufficiently by means of technology that the technology pays for itself—without apparent harm to (indeed, with apparent benefits for!) achievement. It is this question that was the main source of doubt—not the question of whether technology could be used to enhance or individuate instruction.

Choice and Competition

The best available evidence, which is based on comparing students who are randomly "lotteried-in" and attend choice schools to students who are randomly "lotteried-out" and attend traditional public schools, indicates that charter schools and vouchers raise student achievement.[26] Moreover, the typical choice school in the United States—a charter school—has per-pupil spending less than half that of the average traditional public school.[27] Private schools involved in voucher systems also spend far less than the average traditional public school.[28] Thus, the most straightforward look at the facts suggests that choice schools have both higher value-added in achievement and lower costs.

Why should we be unsurprised by this dual attainment, as a logical matter? The answer is that *choice* creates a greater demand for schools that students prefer. *Competition* ensures that the supply side will generate more seats in schools that can efficiently produce what students prefer and fewer seats in schools that produce it inefficiently. That choice must be *combined* with competition is a point missed by many commentators, but it is crucial to the discussion of costs in this paper because it is supply-side forces that ultimately determine schools' productivity and the affordability of education.

Owing to the numerous programs that use the word "choice" without adhering to the basic tenets of the idea, it is worth recalling that all true choice and competition reforms:

1. Attempt to make schools more productive by:
   A. Forcing them to compete for students and the funding that follows them

B. Giving them autonomy to manage how they add value—
    that is, affect students' outcomes

2. Confine government intervention in K–12 education to:

A. Ensuring that schools compete on an even playing field

B. Ensuring that families have accurate information on how
    schools affect students' outcomes (information on *effects,*
    not merely on outcomes)

C. Ensuring that individual students can make the investments
    in their own human capital that will pay off

When a choice and competition reform has a design that imple-
ments these ideals (something that is very feasible but requires
detail beyond the scope of this paper), it gives schools strong incentives to raise their benefit-to-cost ratios and unbinds the constraints
that prevent some schools from doing this now.[29] With better information and funding that follows students, families are more aware
of schools' benefits *and* costs. Since families do not reward schools
for wasting resources on programs that do not benefit their children, schools are under pressure to eliminate unproductive programs, teachers, and work rules. Schools are also under pressure
to adopt innovations that create efficiencies or raise achievement
per dollar spent. Schools can be more productive when families are
able to match their children's educational needs to schools' peda-
gogical strengths.

Because choice and competition represent such a thoroughgoing change in schools' incentives and constraints, we expect to see
schools change on numerous dimensions that raise their benefit-to-
cost ratios. For instance, it should come as no surprise that charter
schools have been pioneers in paying teachers based on their performance and in using the hybrid model of technology in instruction.[30]

Consider a few other ways in which choice schools often manage their budgets differently to produce higher value-added than
traditional public schools do.

First, recognizing that most teachers do not improve their value-added once they have experience of about four years, choice schools frequently employ numerous less-experienced teachers in combination with a "leaven" of highly skilled master teachers who are not only more experienced but who are good at conveying the fruits of their wisdom to the less-experienced teachers. This system allows a choice school to pay teachers in a manner that is highly competitive with traditional public schools and the private sector: there is more money for less-experienced teachers because money is not wasted on giving seniority pay to teachers who are no more productive. This system also allows a choice school to keep highly effective teachers involved in instruction, rather than inducing them to choose an administrative job in which they earn higher salaries but leave teaching.

Second, choice schools often rethink the school year and day. Traditional public schools spend considerable effort ensuring that the number of hours that a teacher is in the classroom is below some amount, that her hours for preparation are above some amount, that the days in the school year are below some amount, and that professional development days are above some amount. In contrast, many choice schools recognize that students' achievement can be *directly* affected by the hours and days they spend on school grounds, in the school's custodial care (not necessarily in instruction), and on fundamental tasks like reading. Thus, it is not unusual to see choice schools experiment with year-round calendars; school days that start early and end late; and school days that contain substantial periods for meals, homework, and play. Choice schools often make these changes pay for themselves by substituting nonteachers for teachers efficiently (when instruction is not going on), by reducing losses associated with students taking books and materials home, and by reducing the need for remediation and disabled instruction.

Third, recognizing that diagnostic assessment is inherently inexpensive (owing to the massive economies of scale associated with modern testing, especially computer-adaptive testing), choice schools often give their students frequent, short assessments that provide near-instant diagnostic information about students' learning gaps. This allows teachers to modify their instruction, revisit confusing topics, and provide remediation in real time. This is in contrast to many traditional public schools that feel so burdened by assessment that they "save it" for the annual state mandatory exam that generates results with such a long lag that they are useless for instructional adjustments in real time. It also appears that traditional public schools are unwilling to move even modest parts of their budgets to assessment (which is cheap but has no natural lobby) and from—say—staff compensation (expensive but has a lobby).

So far I have emphasized the tendency of choice schools to save money or, at least, get more with the same budget. However, there are some items that might cost *more* in a system with true choice and competition. First, we might expect school facilities to need some excess capacity if schools are to shrink and expand with students' demand for them. Second, we might expect additional transportation costs if students are not constrained to attend schools based purely on geographic attendance zones. Third, we might expect some costs associated with making information on schools' effects available to families in a user-friendly way.

Regarding the capacity issue, the areas in which choice programs play the largest role (Washington, DC, New York City, Chicago, and so on) have facilities expenditures that are no higher per pupil than areas in which choice plays no role.[31] As a logical matter, this is because they have re-purposed (often as charter schools) school buildings from which enrollment was draining because families disliked the school in question. However, deliberate systems of re-purposing, which make a great deal of sense, are only needed when existing buildings have exhausted their excess capacity. The most recent, representative data indicate that 59 percent of US schools have excess capacity of at least 5 percent. About

40 percent of schools have excess capacity greater than 20 percent. Thus, the system could easily allow much more flexibility in enrollment than it does currently. Indeed, even among the 18 percent of schools that house more students than they were designed to house, about half are only temporarily "over-enrolled" owing to renovation. And, portable buildings (which often house administrative offices and storage rather than classrooms) have proven to be a highly efficient way of allowing schools to change size smoothly.[32]

School transportation costs in cities—like Washington, DC, New York City, and Chicago—with prevalent choice are not higher on a per-pupil basis than in cities with no choice.[33] However, such cities are not representative of the United States: they are densely populated and have high-coverage systems of public transportation. In order to consider more typical areas, let us compare Pennsylvania and Ohio. These states have comparable shares of their students in private schools and charter schools but Pennsylvania provides school bus transportation for private and charter school students whereas Ohio does not. Yet, Pennsylvania does not spend more per student on school transportation than Ohio does, regardless of whether we adjust for factors like population density.[34] Logically, this is because the vast majority of stops on a school bus route are at points where students are picked up or dropped off, not at schools (which are relatively few, even in an area where choice is prevalent).

Computing schools' value-added and other effects on outcomes may be somewhat beyond the typical person, but making the computations costs a trivial amount relative to education budgets. This is because the computations rely on administrative data that are gathered already. Even the latest value-added evidence, which shows that teachers' value-added can be measured in terms of students' non-academic outcomes (such as attendance and discipline) and long-run outcomes (such as college-going), can be compiled at so little cost that no more than 0.1 percent (*one-tenth* of 1 percent) of a state's total education budget could plausibly be absorbed.[35]

Moreover, providing parents with information on schools costs very little. New York City, in which all prospective ninth graders must submit a preference-ordered list of high schools, is widely recognized for its successful system of informing families about their options, partly through written or online communications and partly through local "choice" centers where families consult individual counselors. Other cities, such as San Francisco, Boston, Charlotte-Mecklenburg, North Carolina, and London, have similar programs to disseminate information. In no case does such a program account for even 0.1 percent of the local education budget. Simply put, disseminating information is very inexpensive. This is because, logically, it is an activity in which there are enormous economies of scale.

Summing up, choice and competition reforms do impose some costs, but they are minor relative to the sources of cost saving—which arise through thoroughgoing incentives to improve productivity.

Virtuous Circles

We have already seen that choice and competition give incentives to schools to be productive—that is, to adopt educational methods that deliver benefits disproportionate to their costs. As a result, we see in practice that choice schools are more likely to reward teachers based on their performance, use technology in hybrid instruction, and so on. But the complementarity between the new methods of improving education goes deeper than such joint adoption.

Fundamentally, all of the new methods we consider in this paper move schools closer to the incentives and rewards that arise in the private sector. Once a school starts down this path, the productivity of various people and inputs becomes much more obvious and many decisions may be reconsidered. In contrast, the command-and-control methods and the arbitrary rewards that currently prevail in the traditional public schools tend to obscure the productivity differences among different policies. As a result, many policies in the traditional public schools do not hold up under benefits-versus-costs scrutiny.

To see this, consider a concrete example. Suppose that a school breaks free from the current system of paying teachers solely on their credentials and seniority and begins to pay them based on their productivity (their effects on students' outcomes, broadly construed). Then, a school may realize that teachers who can work smoothly with technology are able to instruct more students because hybrid classrooms work well for them. Therefore, the school may offer teachers more pay if they show themselves to be apt at hybrid instruction. As a result, the school will tend to fill up with teachers who are good with technology. Those who are not will go elsewhere. But, once the school is filled with technology-enabled teachers, it may realize that it would be productive to invest in even better technology—perhaps technology that allows students to submit homework via computer or that allows teachers to communicate efficiently with parents. With such technology in hand, the school may find it productive to rethink its school day or alter its evaluation system. Perhaps students complete more homework at the school. Perhaps evaluations should be more frequent or problem-based. The point is that once every policy's benefits and costs are considered before it is adopted (or maintained), new methods that improve productivity will be routinely adopted.

Schools that not only increase achievement but do so in the most productive manner create the foundation for skill-based economic growth.

The Need for New Research

The first generation of research on teachers' value-added, technology, and choice focused—for good reason—on simple demonstrations of efficacy. Do teachers actually differ in their value-added? Do they respond at all to rewards? Does some technology raise achievement? Does a student who attends a choice school learn more than one who is lotteried-out? And so on.

Such research plays a crucial role. Without it, policymakers would have little basis for suggesting the expansion of new methods. Nevertheless, the first generation of research typically left the financial side of the methods very vague—partly because the policy trials being analyzed often had arbitrary, even bizarre, financing. For instance, in the few policy trials that exist, the size of rewards for teachers was selected quite arbitrarily—not on a scientific basis designed to maximize the benefits for the costs. Similarly, choice schools are funded in different ways and to different degrees in different cities and states. Often, we can make no sense of why similar states fund their choice schools at such different levels. There are also choice schools that are so poorly funded—for instance, vouchers equal to one-sixth of local per-pupil funding—that it is impossible to extrapolate from their experience to system-wide choice and competition. Schools' technology adoption has often been funded by large federal grants that give schools strong incentives to adopt the technology that is "free" under the grant rather than the technology that would most improve their students' learning.

Indeed, in this paper, we have seen that there is often little research on exactly how pay should change with performance, on how hybrid instruction should be funded, and on exactly what amount of funding should follow each student in a choice and competition environment. Future research needs to fill these gaps for several reasons.

First, reforms that are fundamentally intended to move schools closer to the incentives and constraints of the private sector need to get the finances right. It would be bizarre to say that financial incentives should play an important role, yet the amounts of the incentives should be determined by guessing. Second, policymakers who are fortunate enough to have the support to enact important school reforms often find themselves in a quandary when setting actual amounts. Researchers often help policymakers set up the framework of a new system—for instance, by estimating teachers' value-added—but then beg ignorance when asked for money amounts (such as how much more a teacher should be paid if her value-added is at the ninetieth percentile). The result is that a policy that might work well ends up with a bad financial design and it fails—even though everyone's intentions were good. This often leaves a bad taste, making it harder to enact future reforms. Third, as emphasized in this paper, the new methods of improving schools are all *systemic* methods at heart—that is, they rely on changing incentives and constraints system-wide. To see this, contrast a policy that alters the entire way in which teachers are paid to a policy that introduces a new textbook (a non-systemic method). The new textbook policy will interact in limited ways with other school policies, but the new way of paying teachers will interact with every other important school policy. Because such interactions are important, we need much more information about the financial implications of each policy.

In short, this paper attempts to demonstrate that, with current education budgets, we can afford new methods of improving schools—specifically those that move schools closer to private sector rewards and productivity. However, this demonstration also indicates that we need more research to get those rewards right.

Notes

1. See US Department of Education, "Highlights from PISA 2009: Performance of US 15-Year-Old Students in Reading, Mathematics, and Science Literacy in an International Context," December 2010, http://nces.ed.gov/pubs2011 /2011004.pdf.
2. The inflation adjustment is done using the GDP deflator (US Department of Commerce, Bureau of Economic Analysis, 2012). The GDP deflator is the most appropriate price index for the purpose of comparing education investments to the

US economy as a whole. The other data source is the "Digest of Education Statistics" (US Department of Education, 2012) for total expenditure and average daily attendance in the 1969–70 and 2009–10 school years.

3. These differences are *not* statistically significantly different from zero. Moreover, they are negligible in comparison to a standard deviation on the NAEP (about 30 points) or in comparison to the white-black score gap (29 points). Students who are seventeen years old take the high school versions of the NAEP. The source is the National Assessment of Educational Progress Long Term Trend data tool (US Department of Education, National Center for Education Statistics, 2013).

4. This calculation is based on the persistent teacher effects computed by Douglas Staiger and Jonah Rockoff, "Searching for Effective Teachers with Imperfect Information," *Journal of Economic Perspectives* 24, no. 3 (Summer 2010), 97–118. As they point out, however, their value-added calculations are very similar to those of numerous other researchers who use different data but like methodology. It is important to use shrinkage methods to compute the persistent teacher effect, as opposed to the annual teacher effect which also contains noise from student composition.

5. This calculation is based on National Assessment of Educational Progress individual student data, equated to TIMSS (Trends in International Mathematics and Science Study) data for the latter statement.

6. See Staiger and Rockoff, "Searching for Effective Teachers."

7. See ibid. for a summary of the numerous studies that have demonstrated this point.

8. See Raj Chetty, John Friedman, and Jonah Rockoff, "The Long-term Impacts of Teachers: Teacher Value-added and Student Outcomes in Adulthood," NBER Working Paper 17699, 2011.

9. See Clement Kirabo Jackson, "Non-Cognitive Ability, Test Scores, and Teacher Quality: Evidence from 9th Grade Teachers in North Carolina," NBER Working Paper 18624, 2012.

10. See Thomas J. Kane, Jonah E. Rockoff, and Douglas O. Staiger, "What Does Certification Tell Us About Teacher Effectiveness? Evidence from New York City," *Economics of Education Review* 27, no. 6 (December 2008), 615–631.

11. See Kane, Rockoff, and Staiger, "What Does Certification Tell Us?" and Staiger and Rockoff, "Searching for Effective Teachers."

12. On the former point, see C. Kirabo Jackson and Elias Bruegmann, "Teaching Students and Teaching Each Other: The Importance of Peer Learning for Teachers," *American Economic Journal: Applied Economics* 1, no. 4 (2009), 85–108. On the latter point, see Sally Hudson, "The Effects of Performance-Based Teacher Pay on Student Achievement," SIEPR Discussion Paper 09-023, 2010, Stanford Institute for Economic Policy Research. In addition, there is some evidence that a very well-designed evaluation and feedback system may help teachers improve their value-added: see Eric Taylor and John Tyler, "The Effect of Evaluation on Teacher Performance," *American Economic Review* 102, no. 7 (2012), 3628–51.

13. See Benjamin Scafidi, David Sjoquist, and Todd Stinebrickner, "Do Teachers Really Leave for Higher Paying Jobs in Alternative Occupations?" *The B.E. Journal of Economic Analysis & Policy* 6, no. 1 (2006), 1–44.

14. See Sara Champion, Annalisa Mastri, and Kathryn Shaw, "The Teachers Who Leave: Pulled by Opportunity or Pushed by Accountability?" Stanford University working paper, 2011, available at http://www.rand.org/content/dam/rand/www /external/labor/seminars/allca/Champion-Mastri-Shaw -2011.pdf.

15. Full-time is defined by the US Bureau of Labor Statistics as a nominal 2,080 hours per year, but in fact few of the workers in question are paid on a truly hourly basis or "punch the clock," so their exact hours of work are not relevant or even accurately recorded. Full-time is thus what is usual among workers who define themselves as "full-time" on the jobs in question. They

are at the office more than forty hours in a typical non-vacation week, but they have paid time off in various forms.

16. Author's calculations based on Occupational Employment Statistics, US Bureau of Labor Statistics, 2013.

17. Author's calculations based on the 2009–10 Common Core of Data (US Department of Education, 2013) and the 2009–10 (2010 fiscal year) Public Elementary-Secondary Education Finance Data (US Department of Commerce, 2013).

18. Instructional support staff is defined in Exhibit 1a: School-Level Personnel by the United States Department of Education, Institute of Education Sciences, National Center for Education Statistics, 2013, http://nces.ed.gov/pubs/web/9619ex1a.asp.

19. See Alan Krueger, "Experimental Estimates of Education Production Functions," *Quarterly Journal of Economics* 114, no. 2 (May 1999), 497–532.

20. The best randomized controlled trial of hybrid instruction is currently Linda Cavalluzzo, Deborah Lowther, Christine Mokher, and Xitao Fan, "Effects of the Kentucky Virtual Schools' Hybrid Program for Algebra I on Grade 9 Student Math Achievement" (NCEE 2012-4020) (Washington, DC: National Center for Education Evaluation and Regional Assistance, Institute of Education Sciences, US Department of Education, 2012). However, given the way the study was conducted, it is only useful for assessing the effects on achievement, not the effects on schools' finances. Other studies that examine somewhat similar models of technology use include Lisa Barrow, Lisa Markman, and Cecilia Rouse, "Technology's Edge: The Educational Benefits of Computer-Aided Instruction," *American Economic Journal: Economic Policy* 1, no. 1 (2009), 52–74; and Larisa Campuzano, Mark Dynarski, Roberto Agodini, and Kristina Rall, "Effectiveness Of Reading And Mathematics Software Products: Findings From Two Student Cohorts" (NCEE 2009-4041), (Washington, DC: US Department of Education, Institute of Education Sciences, National Center for Education Evaluation and Regional Assistance, 2009).

21. This is not to say that the use of technology to enhance instruction is rare in public schools. According to the latest nationally representative study of teachers' use of technology in instruction, at least half of teachers claim to use technology on a frequent basis for activities such as problem-solving, drills, practice of basic skills, and preparing text. However, it appears that almost none of these teachers are in schools that deliberately substitute technology for teacher time. See Lucinda Gray, Nina Thomas, and Laurie Lewis, "Teachers' Use of Educational Technology in US Public Schools: 2009" (NCES 2010-040) (Washington, DC, National Center for Education Statistics, Institute of Education Sciences, US Department of Education, 2010).

22. See Rocketship Education, "Annual Report to the Santa Clara County Office and Board of Education," January 2013, http://www.sccoe.org/supoffice/innovative-schools /Charter%20School%20Annual%20Reports/Rocketship %20Education.pdf.

23. These financial data are for the 2009–10 school year. For sources, see the next note.

24. Rocketship 2009–10 school year financial data are from Rocketship Education, "Rocketship Education and its Affiliates: Consolidated Audited Financial Statements for the Year Ended June 30, 2010," https://rsed.box.com/shared/z3kxe9iuoo. All enrollment data are based on the 2009–10 Common Core of Data. Traditional public schools' financial data are from the 2009–10 (2010 fiscal year) Public Elementary-Secondary Education Finance Data.

25. It is extremely difficult to compare charter and traditional public schools' capital expenditures because they are financed so differently, especially for charter management organizations that are starting up new schools.

26. See, for instance, Caroline Hoxby and Jonah Rockoff, "Findings from the City of Big Shoulders: Students Learn More in Chicago Charter Schools," *Education Next* 5, no. 4 (Fall 2005); Caroline Hoxby and Sonali Murarka, "How New York

City's Charter Schools Affect Achievement," *Education Next* 8, no. 3 (Summer 2008); Joshua Angrist, Sarah Cohodes, Susan Dynarski, Jon B. Fullerton, Thomas J. Kane, Parag Pathak, and Christopher Walters, "Student Achievement in Massachusetts' Charter Schools," Center for Education Policy Research at Harvard University, 2011; Joshua Angrist, Sarah Cohodes, Susan Dynarski, Parag Pathak, and Christopher Walters, "Stand and Deliver: Post-Secondary Outcomes at Boston's Charter High Schools," MIT manuscript, 2013.

27. Author's calculations based on matching the 2009–10 Common Core of Data (US Department of Education, 2013) to the 2009–10 (2010 fiscal year) Public Elementary-Secondary Education Finance Data (US Department of Commerce, 2013). The former dataset is the source of student enrollment data. The latter dataset is the source of expenditure data.

28. Author's calculations based on Internal Revenue Service, Statistics of Income Division, "Exempt Organizations Business Master File Extract," 2013; and on US Department of Education, National Center for Education Statistics, "Schools and Staffing Survey, 2007–08."

29. I do not emphasize the liberating effect of choice and competition reforms on the constraints that apparently bind many traditional public schools: work rules, union contracts, state and federal mandates, and the like. The reason is that many of these constraints are essentially self-imposed because schools have had weak or no incentives to oppose them. That is, any given principal can legitimately complain that he or she is bound by current work rules, but the system of traditional public education *chose* these work rules in negotiations with staff over a long period in which incentives to be productive were extremely weak.

30. See Hoxby and Murarka, "How New York City's Charter Schools Affect Achievement."

31. Author's calculations based on the 2009–10 (2010 fiscal year) "Public Elementary-Secondary Education Finance Data" (US Department of Commerce, 2013).

32. The source of the facilities statistics in this paragraph is Bradford Chaney and Laurie Lewis, "Public School Principals Report on Their School Facilities: Fall 2005" (NCES 2007-007), US Department of Education (Washington, DC: National Center for Education Statistics, 2007).

33. Author's calculations based on the 2009–10 (2010 fiscal year) "Public Elementary-Secondary Education Finance Data" (US Department of Commerce, 2013).

34. The adjustments make little difference in any case, owing to the similarity between Ohio's and Pennsylvania's districts in terms of student density, school size, and the like. Actually, Pennsylvania spends slightly less per student than Ohio does on school transportation, but the difference is too small to be interpretable.

35. These numbers are based on the *actual* costs of such computations as made by researchers working with districts' and states' administrative data, including data on non-test-score outcomes such as studied by Chetty et al., "Long-term Impacts of Teachers," and by Clement Kirabo Jackson, "Non-Cognitive Ability, Test Scores, and Teacher Quality."

CHAPTER 10

Relying on Evidence

Grover "Russ" Whitehurst

For most of our history the pace of cultural learning was slow, with one generation's experiences not very different from those of their forebears. But that pace is now accelerating so rapidly that the older members of overlapping generations have grown up in circumstances that are outside the experience of younger people. My grandparents lived most of their lives without antibiotics, television, commercial aviation, supermarkets, computers, and almost everything else we consider modern.

Some accounts of the explosion of knowledge and technology in fields such as health care, transportation, and communication credit the inventions in those fields for progress while paying no attention to the processes that made those inventions possible. There is a fundamental sense in which the incandescent light bulb was invented and that shared act of creation is part of the story of cultural evolution. But the translation of that invention into something utilitarian that altered how our planet looks from space was the product of experimentation by Thomas Edison's team at Menlo Park.

Experiments with physical materials such as those carried out by Edison must have had precursors that are prehistoric—imagine a Paleolithic man discovering which rocks produce sparks when struck together. Indeed, nearly all animal species are capable of at least rudimentary forms of trial-and-error learning. But what is simple when a cause that lies within an animal's behavioral repertoire is quickly and reliably followed by an effect the animal values becomes opaque when the effect is multiply determined, probabilistic, and delayed. So whereas an architect of viaducts in ancient Greece would likely have been able to understand the trial-and-error process by which Edison determined that carbon made the best light filament, neither would have been equipped by virtue of their training and experience to understand how to find out whether physical exercise affects health. Nor would either have been well-equipped to determine whether the placement of an advertisement on a page increases sales, or the training of teachers affects their effectiveness, or any other cause-effect relationship that can only be discerned through the application of methods that are capable of extracting a cause-and-effect signal from the noise of weakly probabilistic relationships.

These methods of experimenting to discover complex and probabilistic relationships are recent cultural inventions. Fields that have embraced them have shown rapid progress. Fields that have not, most certainly including education, have stood still.

James Lind's research on treating scurvy among British sailors, carried out in 1747, is generally credited as the first recorded instance of the application of a quasi-experimental design to study an intervention's impact. Lind selected twelve sailors stricken with scurvy, divided them into six groups of two, and gave each group a different dietary treatment. Those given oranges and lemons improved quickly whereas those otherwise treated, e.g., with vinegar, did not. Many aspects of modern experimental design and analysis were missing in Lind's approach. For example, he did not randomly assign subjects to treatment conditions and did not quantify or test for the significance of the difference in outcomes between groups. Nevertheless, his approach of systematic variation of treatment and observation of results is the foundation of systematic learning through trial and error.

It was 1925 before Ronald Fisher, in his book *Statistical Methods for Research Workers,* explicated the critical role of randomization in assigning subjects to treatments and addressed the need for statistics to deal with error and variability in results. Fisher's methods were developed for use in agricultural and genetic research, but their extension to medicine and the social sciences was straightforward, if not immediate.

The randomized controlled trial of streptomycin for bronchial tuberculosis, begun in Great Britain in 1947, was the first well-implemented and documented randomized trial involving human subjects. The amount of streptomycin was limited so that it was ethically acceptable for the control subjects to be untreated by the drug. Randomization was used instead of the traditional technique of subject assignment to condition by alternation in order to conceal the allocation schedule from those who might bias selection into condition and from those reading the X-rays collected from patients. Procedures and results were meticulously documented. It remains a touchstone for experimental designs in general.

The use of experimental approaches to determine what works has proliferated in health care, industrial production, psychology, and business since their introduction in agriculture and medicine in the first half of the twentieth century. Jim Manzi, who runs a company that carries out experimental trials for business, asserts that many leading companies are relentless experimenters.[1] For example, Google carries out over twelve thousand experiments a year, about 10 percent of which lead to changes in business practices. CapitalOne (a leading credit card company) runs over sixty thousand experiments a year, to which it attributes its growth and competitive edge. Manzi quotes a manager at Harrah's Casino in Las Vegas as saying that there are three things that could cost a manager his job there: harassing women, stealing from the company, and not having a control group.

During the time in the twentieth century in which other fields were embracing systematic experimentation as the fundamental process for learning what works, education was pre-scientific.

In 1971, the President's Commission on School Finance commissioned the Rand Corporation to review research on what was known about what works in education, reasoning, "The wise expenditure of public funds for education . . . must be based on knowledge of which investments produce results, and which do not." Rand concluded:

> The body of educational research now available leaves much to be desired, at least by comparison with the level of understanding that has been achieved in numerous other fields. . . . Research has found nothing that consistently and unambiguously makes a difference in student outcomes.

Almost thirty years later, in 1999, the National Academies of Science came to essentially the same conclusion:

> One striking fact is that the complex world of education—unlike defense, health care, or industrial production—does not rest on a strong research base. In no other field are personal experience and ideology so frequently relied on to make policy choices, and in no other field is the research base so inadequate and little used.

In comparison to the sad state of affairs that existed heretofore, the twenty-first century has seen an explosion of rigorous and relevant research, providing for the first time a foundation for evidence-based education, which is the use of the best currently available empirical evidence in making policy and practice decisions in education. Evidence-based education requires a supply of evidence that is relevant to policy and practice, methods for vetting the quality of evidence, processes for synthesis and dissemination of research findings, and demand for evidence among practitioners and policymakers. Substantial progress has occurred in each of these areas, although demand lags behind supply because competitive pressures that create incentives to adopt more effective practices are relatively weak in education compared to many other fields.

The Institute of Education Sciences (IES) within the US Department of Education has played an important role on the supply side of evidence-based education. IES was established in 2002 with the mission of producing rigorous and relevant research to support education policy and practice. Under IES the federal government for the first time established a clear set of priorities for education research funding, articulated standards for research quality that emphasized the validity of causal claims, created a set of processes for research grant competitions that were orderly, predictable, and grounded on systematic peer review, and garnered a budget from Congress that was sufficient to fund nearly all grant applications that were deemed by peer reviewers to be of the highest quality. IES also launched rigorous evaluations of federal education programs, funded university-based doctoral training programs in the education sciences, and directed hundreds of millions of dollars toward the establishment of statewide longitudinal databases of student and teacher records that could be grist to the mill of education research. Through its What Works Clearinghouse (WWC), IES took responsibility for vetting and disseminating findings from studies on the effectiveness of individual programs and practices, as well as publishing practice guides in which consensus panels synthesize recommendations for practitioners from the existing research base.

In part because of the investments and focus of IES, a new community of researchers has arisen that is committed to conducting rigorous and relevant research on education. The community includes people who had been doing rigorous and relevant research in education for the whole of their careers, but often in isolation from others doing such work in education. It also includes those with established careers in cognate fields such as psychology and economics who shifted their attention to education and significant and growing numbers of newly minted researchers trained in interdisciplinary doctoral programs in education science who are grounded in the normative canons of the social, behavioral, and cognitive sciences.

Progress in Knowledge of What Works

Considerable progress has been made in identifying particular programs and practices that have an impact on student achievement.

The What Works Clearinghouse (WWC) has been in operation for almost a decade with the goal of being the central and trusted source of scientific evidence for what works in education. To date the WWC has conducted systematic reviews of 9,325 research studies, of which 654 were determined to either meet all methodological standards or meet standards with reservations. These rigorous studies enabled the WWC to identify 105 separate interventions with positive effects on student outcomes within the domains of literacy, mathematics, science, student behavior, dropout prevention, early childhood education, English language learners, and students with disabilities. This is a far cry from the conclusions of Rand over forty years ago that research has found nothing that consistently makes a difference in student outcomes.

Progress in Knowledge of What Makes a Difference

The WWC examines the impact of branded interventions that are intended to affect student outcomes. Meanwhile, a different body of research employs different methods that address the influence of the organization and process by which education is delivered. The preferred method for studies of what works is the carefully planned and executed randomized trial. Typical methods for studies of what makes a difference are epidemiological, i.e., they involve an examination of naturally occurring patterns of association among input and output variables in education. The difference in methodological approach between studies of what works vs. studies of what makes a difference is not so much a matter of choice as of necessity. Whereas discrete interventions lend themselves readily to carefully planned and implemented experiments and quasi-experiments, the broader governance arrangements in which education is delivered and the types of policies decided by district, state, and federal officials are usually difficult to vary experimentally. They often need to be evaluated post-hoc because they are instituted with no thought to their evaluation. As state- and district-level longitudinal education databases have come online in the last decade, the field of education epidemiology has grown by leaps and bounds, both in the volume of published work and in methodological sophistication.

Consider the question of how much teachers, schools, and districts matter to student outcomes. Thinking on this topic through the 1990s was heavily influenced by the landmark 1966 report, *Equality of Educational Opportunity*, by sociologist James Coleman. This was a huge study employing sixty thousand teachers in grade six and beyond in over three thousand schools. The principal finding was that nearly all of the variability in what students achieved was attributable to their socioeconomic background rather than to their schools and teachers. On the subject of teachers, Coleman wrote, "A list of variables concerning such matters as teachers' scores on a vocabulary test, their own level of education, their years of experience, showed little relation to achievement. . . ."

Coleman's insight that schools should be evaluated on their outcomes, not their resources, and his attempt to do so scientifically

FIGURE 1. Comparison of One Standard Deviation of Teacher/Classroom, School, and District Differences on Student Achievement*

(* 0.10 of a student standard deviation = roughly 25% of a school year of learning)

were major advances in education research. But his methods are now understood to have been flawed. All of his analyses were conducted on data that had been aggregated to the school level. For example, the average vocabulary score for all teachers in a school was related to the average test score for all children in a school. We now have available statistical methods that are able to isolate the influence of different levels of the education system on student outcomes. These multilevel approaches generate very different conclusions from those that were the received wisdom of the last century.

Fig. 1 represents the results from a recent study based on statewide data on fourth and fifth grade student achievement in reading and mathematics from North Carolina and Florida for the 2008–2009 school year.[2] It addresses the relative influence of teachers, schools, and classrooms by mapping each to a common unit of a standard deviation of difference in student achievement. One way to think about a standard deviation is that it corresponds to a difference between roughly the thirtieth and seventieth percentiles of performance. Thus, based on the data represented in the figure, students in a classroom with a teacher at the seventieth percentile would be about 0.16 standard deviation ahead of students in the classroom of a teacher at the thirtieth percentile, which is nearly 40 percent of a school year. As indicated in the figure, the impact of schools and districts is less than that of teachers, but still a difference of months of a school year.

We now know that teachers, schools, and districts matter for student achievement, i.e., that demographics and family background are not everything. However, we have not yet translated this understanding into the design and implementation of interventions that can be shown to improve student achievement. It is as if Edison demonstrated that there was variation in the efficacy of light bulb filaments but never got to the point of identifying a practical design. In other words, we know what makes a difference but not what works.

A Look to the Future

Never make predictions, especially about the future.
—Casey Stengel

The transformation of education from a field based on intuition, historical practice, and fad and fancy to a field based on evidence has been thwarted until recently by an inadequate supply of rigorous and relevant research. The supply side of evidence-based education has advanced rapidly in the last decade. But demand is still weak.

The essential question for those interested in the advance of evidence-based education is whether demand is weak because there is something wrong with the research that is being provided or because there is something about the way the field of education is organized that suppresses the market for evidence-based approaches. The problem lies in both areas.

The research and development enterprise in education needs to invest more deeply and systematically in process innovations that will serve the practical needs of school districts and schools. We are unlikely to get dramatically better at educating students until we have a cadre of researchers whose job is to engineer more efficient and effective processes for carrying out the work of schools. Education has an increasingly strong research community, but it lacks more than a few people trained and employed to improve the workaday processes of delivering education through systematic experimentation.

If Harrah's intends to increase the number of its mid-week customers from Southern California through the mailing of a discount offer, the person responsible for designing the solicitation will lose his job if there isn't a control group. If Google wants to find the display size for search results that generates the most click-throughs on smart phones, it will systematically vary that parameter across different randomly selected groups of users. It has employees and contractors to design the intervention and analyze the results. Its business success depends on finding the best answer.

In contrast, if a large school district wants to redesign its processes for recruiting new teachers by changing when applications are due and offers of employment are made, it would be exceedingly rare if it either had anyone on staff or could find anyone in a local university who would be interested and able to carry out an experiment on the issue. The education research community, which is predominantly comprised of academics, is not interested in such atheoretical, small-bore questions. But these are the types of issues that education administrators address, whereas broad questions of education policy seldom are within their bailiwick. And because the managers of schools and school districts have rarely if ever been supplied with research that directly addresses the decisions they have to make, they have not had the opportunity to develop an appetite for evidence-based education.

Those who have responsibility for the supply of education research, including universities and funding agencies, need to create a pipeline that is primed with practical research of immediate relevance to everyday education decisions. This will require not only a redirection of the goal of much education research but also much better access by the research community to the administrative data at the state, district, and school level on which the research would draw. It will also require a new channel of federal funding for short-term projects that are of immediate practical significance and that can be reviewed and funded within a few months. This is in contrast to the current modus operandi in which applications for research grants can take a year or more to make their way through the review system and are typically for multiyear projects.

Whether a supply of immediately practical research findings will increase demand for evidence-based education is an empirical question. I expect it would be useful but that its impact would be muted by the same factors that suppress that uptake of evidence that already exists on the impact of broader policies and programs.

The reason that businesses such as Google, Harrah's, and CapitalOne have an appetite for evidence of what works is that avoidable errors in their business decisions go directly to their bottom line, for which managers at many levels and the CEOs are accountable. Google needs to figure out how to maintain its search dominance on mobile devices or others will take its market share. There are lots of casinos in Las Vegas. Harrah's success depends on competing successfully for customers. And so on.

Education, in contrast, is by and large a public monopoly. A recruitment process for new teachers that is much less effective than it might be does not result in the school district losing students or revenue, at least not within a time span or through a series of events that would make the connection discernible. A truly dysfunctional management process may call attention to itself and the administrator responsible for it, but there is no incentive built into the system to experiment with improvements in processes that seem to be OK.

The most powerful way to incentivize evidence-based decision-making in education would be a system of delivery in which schools compete for students and their funding and in which the jobs and compensation of school employees and managers are conditional on their success in attracting and retaining students. Until errors in decision-making have palpable consequences for those responsible for those decisions, the demand for evidence that will enable better decisions will be weak.

In short, the education research community needs to prime the pump of evidence-based education with a supply of research findings that are of immediate relevance to workaday decision-making, e.g., recruiting tools that enhance the effectiveness of the workforce; ways to increase the productivity of the central office; and differences in the impact of available curriculum materials for particular types of teachers and students. If this is to have more than marginal impact, it will need to be accompanied by a redesign of the delivery of education services such that schools and those who work in them are subject to market forces.

The nation can no longer tolerate vast differences in the quality of its schools and classrooms. Residential geography and quirks of school choice and classroom assignment cannot continue to define the education destiny of individual students. We need for all of our schools to be good enough to do the job that is expected of them. This will require nothing less than a relentless effort to engineer processes that assure the best possible outcomes and that result in continuous improvement. Much of this work will be down in the weeds and the results of any single effort will be incremental. Examined within a short time frame, those results may not look like they are going very far. But it is the accumulation and progression of those incremental improvements that will ultimately be transformational for student achievement and the nation's future.

Evidence-based education has shown progress over the last decade that seemed unimaginable twenty years ago. A foundation is in place for the kind of explosive growth in knowledge and application of what works that has been seen in other fields. Improvements in the relevance of the supply of research and the incentives for educators to make the best possible decisions are the necessary ingredients for the next stage of the reform of our education system.

Notes

1. Jim Manzi, *Uncontrolled: The Surprising Payoff of Trial-and-Error for Business, Politics, and Society* (New York: Basic Books, 2012).

2. Grover J. "Russ" Whitehurst, Matthew M. Chingos, and Michael R. Gallaher, "Do School Districts Matter?" (Washington, DC: Brookings Institution Press, 2013), http://www.brookings.edu/~/media/research/files/papers/2013/3/27-school-district-impacts-whitehurst/districts_report_03252013_web.pdf.

CHAPTER 11

Educating Smart Kids, Too

Chester E. Finn Jr.

The United States has made remarkable progress in providing all its children with access to education, but it hasn't been easy and it hasn't yet been enough. Getting youngsters inside the doors of acceptable schools is only the beginning. To give them a well-aimed shot at the American dream, they need to acquire a full measure of knowledge and skills, which introduces issues of educational quality and effectiveness as well as access and equity. On these dimensions, we still have a considerable distance to travel. And the most recent group of kids to turn up as victims of education that's less than they (and the nation) need is gifted students, particularly those with high potential but low family incomes.

The Access Agenda

The access trajectory is relatively easy to trace. In the country's early days, primary-secondary education was essentially a private good, available to youngsters whose parents cared about—and could afford—it. For the most part, that meant boys from relatively prosperous families.

Beginning in New England as early as the seventeenth century, however, towns started to take upon themselves the responsibility of providing a semblance of "public" education to the children who lived there, mostly at the primary level and often still limited to boys. It was optional for families and, of course, it varied greatly in quality.

In the 1840s, Massachusetts began to make primary education a state responsibility. Other states followed, as did compulsory attendance laws, though initially these required children to attend school for just a few years.

Publicly funded high schools were the next stage. But universal attendance in them was neither required nor expected until after World War II—which is also when the United States began to fixate on high school dropout rates.

That sluggishness, however, was not a product of exclusion or parsimony so much as a corollary of an economy that for many years did fine without everyone acquiring a secondary education. Basic civic participation and parenting required near-universal literacy, but factory and farm work did not really demand the skills and knowledge that we associate with high school. So secondary schooling was long the preserve of those headed toward college and into the kinds of careers that called for it. Hence, as high school participation widened, so did the practice of multiple curricular tracks such that some students followed the college prep sequence while others took vocational classes. Still others were cast into a sort of educational no-man's-land called the general track.

Even as K–12 education gradually became universalized, however, access to decent school opportunities remained a problem for many.

The Supreme Court began to tackle one of the biggest challenges with its *Brown v. Board of Education* ruling in 1954, which commenced the dismantling of racial segregation. The following two decades brought a cascade of federal court orders, laws, rules, and programs in the "civil rights" and "compensatory education" realms as well as the requirement that handicapped youngsters (today we say "children with disabilities") be afforded a "free, appropriate" public education rather than the attics and inferior offerings to which many had been confined. Additional legislation sought to provide suitable courses of study for recent immigrants (bilingual education) and to lower barriers that were believed to constrain educational opportunities for low-income children, homeless youngsters—and girls.

Many of these initiatives created unintended problems and few, if any, achieved all that they set out to do. But there is no denying that the pursuit of "educational equity," as it came to be known, was the dominant preoccupation of American K–12 education from 1954 until 1983.

The Pursuit of Excellence

Then came *A Nation at Risk*, the clarion declaration by the National Commission on Excellence in Education that the United States faced a bleak future if it did not pull up its socks and pursue quality and performance in its schools with at least as much vigor as access and equality.

This was not a total surprise. Several other reports and studies that emerged in the early 1980s contained similar warnings. And a few voices (my own included) had been cautioning for some time that American education was going overboard on access while neglecting results; that it had allowed "equality" to be mis-defined; and that it was substituting intentions, rules, programs, and expenditures for evidence of actual learning.

A gradual shifting of gears and priorities commenced, led mostly by governors, many of them in the South, who had determined that the future prosperity of their states hinged on getting greater skills and knowledge into many more children's heads than their current school systems were producing. (I was then living in Nashville, where I heard Governor Lamar Alexander declare perhaps a hundred times to various audiences that "Better schools mean better jobs for Tennesseans.")

They knew, however—as the great social scientists James Coleman, Christopher Jencks, and Daniel P. Moynihan had been pointing out for years—that simply pumping additional resources into the existing system would not yield better results. They knew that much must change in a system that was loath to change. And so they embarked on multiple efforts—invariably resisted by the education establishment and its myriad interest groups—to alter that system in spite of itself.

We haven't space enough to describe in depth the many elements of the "excellence movement," as it came to be known. Suffice it to say that it focused—and still does—on setting actual academic standards that students and schools are supposed to achieve; creating reliable measures of performance that are based on results; devising accountability regimens by which incentives induce stronger achievement and interventions are put in place where it flags; providing families with choices among multiple schools while broadening the definition of schools to include charter schools, then "virtual" and "hybrid" schools and much else; strengthening school leadership; ensuring that classrooms are staffed by able, well-prepared, pedagogically competent instructors; and boosting both the quality and the results-based accountability of teachers, principals, and others whose job it is to educate children.

Equity + Excellence?

The push for excellence did not displace America's concern with equity. We struggle mightily in the abstract with former Health, Education and Welfare Secretary John Gardner's old question of whether we can be equal and excellent, too. But in the real world of K–12 education policy, these twin reform impulses were more-or-less combined in such ambitious undertakings as Bill Clinton's "Goals 2000" act, George W. Bush's "No Child Left Behind" law, and Barack Obama's "Race to the Top" program. Stronger achievement was the goal, but that goal was pursued mainly by setting minimum standards of proficiency and narrowing achievement gaps. Nor did any of the special programs and provisions for disabled, low-income, and non-English-speaking pupils go away.

The upshot: our pursuit of excellence has served primarily to benefit the same demographic segments for whom access to a decent education had long posed the greatest difficulty.

This is no bad thing for America. This emphasis on basic proficiency for everyone could even be described as completing the equity agenda. For many of these kids, it has begun to do measurable good. True, overall test scores and graduation rates are still nowhere near where they should be and our secondary schools are mostly still far from satisfactory (and some are truly abysmal). Still, the past decade or two have witnessed measurable gains by younger students, particularly in math and especially among populations that had the farthest to go.

This is worthy, surely, of a sincere huzzah. But we're a long way from three cheers, both because progress has been halting and modest even for those making it and because we've failed to pay suitable attention to students (and schools) that are already above the "proficient bar," yet far from achieving all they could.

The Education Outcasts of 2014

Barack Obama and Mitt Romney both attended elite private high schools, as did George W. Bush, Al Gore, and John Kerry. Both are undeniably smart and well-educated and owe much of their success to the strong foundation laid by excellent schools. Every motivated, high-potential young American deserves a similar opportunity. But the majority of smart kids lack the wherewithal to enroll in rigorous private schools. They depend on public education to prepare them for life. Yet American public education is failing to create enough opportunities for hundreds of thousands of these high-potential girls and boys.

In Ohio alone, some 250,000 current pupils—about 15 percent of all children in public education there—have been identified by their school districts as "gifted" (using the several metrics that the Buckeye State employs for this purpose, including superior "visual or performing arts ability"). Yet barely one-fifth of these youngsters actually receive "gifted education services" from their schools. (Such services take various forms but most commonly involve separate classrooms with more challenging curricula and specially prepared teachers, at least for core academic subjects.)

Imagine the outcry across the land if just one in five children identified as "disabled" was receiving "special education services" from his school!

Yet gifted youngsters are widely neglected. Because they're already above the "proficient bar" in academic achievement at a time when most federal and state policies are fixed on boosting low achievers over that bar, schools and teachers have little incentive to focus on their educational needs or to devote resources to their schooling. And if we can extrapolate from the Ohio data—that state accounts for about 3.7 percent of all K–12 students in the land—the United States may contain as many as six million high-ability youngsters whom it is not educating to the max. (The National Association for Gifted Children estimates about half that number. The fact that nobody really knows also attests to the vagueness of these definitions and to disputation even among advocates as to what exactly qualifies as giftedness.)

This neglect isn't just a matter of fairness and equal opportunity for kids. It's also a matter of long-term societal well-being.

America's ability to compete economically on a shrinking planet, as well as our national security and cultural vitality, depends to a great extent on whether today's ablest girls and boys are well-prepared to become tomorrow's scientists, inventors, entrepreneurs, engineers, and civic leaders. Yes, it's important to impart proficiency to every young person in the land. But it's at least as important to equip those likely to be the next generation's pathbreakers with all the learning they can absorb. Our education system at every level needs to view human capital development more comprehensively than it has. The system also needs to be able to "walk and chew gum at the same time," i.e., to tackle the challenge of underachievement even as it devotes concentrated attention to youngsters with enormous high-end potential.

Compared with the rest of the world—at least the parts we're most apt to compete with—we're not doing this very well. Roughly 6 percent of US students score at the advanced level in core subjects on the National Assessment of Educational Progress. When this is equated to other countries via the Organisation for Economic Co-operation and Development's Programme for International Student Assessment (PISA), we find (in math, for the high school graduating class of 2009) that sixteen other nations had at least twice as large a fraction of their fifteen-year-olds scoring at that level. World leader Taiwan was at 28 percent but even Germany clocked in around 13 percent. (To their credit, several US states, led by Massachusetts, did notably better than the American average. Ohio—discussed above—was just a hair above that average. In the spirit of rising tides lifting boats, states that did well overall also generally showed gains at the high and low ends of the achievement distribution.[1])

Most apt to be neglected are those who are smart but poor. Upper-middle-class families with educated parents, by and large, do an acceptable job of steering their high-ability daughters and sons through the education maze. It's surely possible for smart kids to get a strong education in today's America—but most of the time that requires adults in their lives who are education-minded, ambitious, pushy, well-enough connected (and confident enough) to "work the system" and, in many cases, to buy their way into private schools or posh suburban districts.

Smart *poor* kids seldom have those assets at home. They are generally educated not according to how much they could learn but according to the norms of the public schools in their neighborhoods. Since these are usually poor neighborhoods, the schools are apt to concentrate energies and resources on the large numbers of students below the proficient line.

Poor parents may not know what their children are capable of and probably lack the resources to purchase supplemental courses, educational software, weekend and summer programs, and much else that similarly gifted youngsters from more prosperous circumstances are apt to have showered upon them.

One consequence, as economist Caroline Hoxby and colleagues have shown, is that high-ability, high-achieving youngsters from poor and minority backgrounds tend not even to *apply* to the country's elite colleges and universities, although they could likely gain admission, obtain financial aid, and thrive academically.[2]

A Four-Part Problem

Today's systemic failure takes four main forms:

1. We're weak at identifying "gifted and talented" children early unless their parents push for it. Without early identification, youngsters are apt to lose out on opportunities to accelerate, to get into such special classrooms and supplemental programs as do exist, to enroll in magnet or charter schools designed to challenge them, and to gain access (when they reach high school) to Advanced Placement courses, International Baccalaureate programs, and other offerings that typically presuppose a solid education in the early grades. Those that do get

spotted and invited into gifted and talented classes and such are less apt to be poor and members of minority groups. In Ohio, for example, where 48 percent of all public-school students qualify as "economically disadvantaged," among those flagged as gifted that figure is 21 percent. As for race, while 18 percent of white youngsters in the Buckeye state are deemed gifted, along with a whopping 28 percent of Asian students, that's true of just 5 percent of black pupils and 6 percent of Hispanic children.

2. We don't have enough gifted-education classrooms and specialized schools (with suitable teachers and curricula) to serve even the existing demand, much less what might be induced by more thorough talent identification. Faced with budget crunches and federal and state pressure to close achievement gaps and turn around awful schools, many districts are cutting their advanced classes. In political, policy, and philanthropic circles alike, educating high-potential children ranks low on the priority list. It seems faintly elitist—and there's a widespread belief that "these kids will do fine anyway."

3. Surprisingly little is known about what strategies, structures, and programs work best in educating high-ability youngsters. Educators and parents alike tend to assume that if it carries the "gifted" label or is academically selective at the front end, it must be effective. Yet the (all too meager) research and evaluation that have been conducted in this realm—both in the United States and overseas—yield a mixed picture when it comes to the academic "value added" by gifted-and-talented programs and selective-admission schools. This poses a challenge for scholars, advocates, and policymakers alike, a challenge that is deepened by the immense variability of programs dubbed "gifted" within American public education.[3]

4. When students finally reach high school, especially if they live in poor neighborhoods, they may find just a smattering of honors or AP classes, nothing like the ample course offerings of well-resourced suburban districts and elite private schools.[4]

Some public high schools do focus exclusively on high-ability, highly motivated students. But when Jessica Hockett and I searched for them in connection with a Hoover-Fordham study that led to our book, *Exam Schools,* we found just 165 that met our criteria within a public-school universe of more than 20,000 high schools.[5] These specialized institutions educate about 1 percent of students. Nineteen states have none. Only three big cities have more than five such schools (Los Angeles has zero). Almost all of these schools have far more qualified applicants than they can accommodate. Hence they practice selective admissions, turning away thousands of students who could benefit from what they have to offer. Northern Virginia's acclaimed Thomas Jefferson High School for Science and Technology, for example, receives about 3,300 applicants a year—two-thirds of them academically qualified—for 480 places.

Many such schools are urban—a few are even statewide residential schools—and they're free, making them terrific opportunities for high-ability youngsters from straitened circumstances. Critics call them elitist, but we found the opposite. These are great schools accessible to families who can't afford private alternatives or pricey suburbs. We learned that 37 percent of their pupils qualify for the federal subsidized lunch program, almost the same as the 39 percent in the national public high school population.

The schools we studied, by and large, are educational oases for families with smart kids but few alternatives. They're safe havens, too—schools where everyone focuses on teaching and learning, not maintaining order. Yes, they even have sports teams, but their orchestras are better. Yes, some have had to crack down on cheating, but in these schools it's fine to be a nerd. You're surrounded by kids like you—some smarter than you—and taught by capable teachers who welcome the challenge, teachers more apt to have doctorates or experience at the university level than high school instructors elsewhere. You aren't searched for weapons at the door.

And you're pretty sure to graduate and go on to a good college. Many more students could benefit from schools like these—and the numbers would multiply if our education system did right by such youngsters in the early grades. But that will happen only when we acknowledge that leaving no child behind means paying as much attention to those who've mastered the basics—and have the capacity and motivation for much more—as we do to those who cannot yet read or subtract.

It's time to end the bias in American education against gifted and talented pupils and quit assuming that every school must be all things to all students, a simplistic formula that ends up neglecting all sorts of girls and boys, many of them poor and minority, who would benefit from more challenging classes and schools. Smart kids shouldn't have to go to private schools or get turned away from Bronx Science or Thomas Jefferson simply because there's no room for them.

The Role of Research & Advocacy

Even getting the "gifted student problem" onto the policy radar screen is a heavy lift, due to its political incorrectness and the belief that smart kids don't need special attention. Because upper-middle-class parents, as noted above, often succeed at navigating the education system on behalf of their own progeny, the loudest "squeaky wheel" doesn't squeak very loudly—and, when it does, it sounds like special pleading on behalf of the already privileged. Though states have advocacy organizations on behalf of gifted and talented education—loosely joined under the National Association for Gifted Children—mostly they agitate for more money and do so in old-fashioned ways. This is not a sophisticated, modern lobbying operation.

Despite all the alarm over international economic competitiveness, essentially nobody in Washington—certainly nobody at the Education Department or White House—is paying attention to this problem (save for boosting science, technology, engineering, and math—the STEM cluster—though not necessarily for smart kids).

Nor have the business and scientific communities made it a priority. They are likelier to focus on immigration laws that determine the difficulty of importing advanced talent from abroad.

One might expect higher education leaders to focus on this issue, but the elite universities have plenty of smart, qualified applicants—huge proportions of them from the upper middle class, of course—and many other campuses accept all who apply, then "remediate" them as needed.

Into this vacuum have come a handful of scholars, studies, think tanks, and private funders. Research undertaken at Brookings, Hoover, the Thomas B. Fordham Institute, and the American Psychological Association has documented the problem. International assessments have added worrisome statistics. *Education Next* has published revealing articles. Individual scholars with strong track records of research, analysis, and advocacy in this realm include at least half the members of the Hoover Institution's Koret Task Force on K–12 Education. And a few private funders—perhaps most notably the Kern Family Foundation—have helped with these and other endeavors.

But much heavy lifting lies ahead and the think tank world is probably best situated to engage in it. This isn't the sort of politically correct topic that professors of education favor; when it's docketed for discussion at national education-research symposia and conclaves of private funders, such sessions draw sparse attendance. It is, in fact, particularly well-suited to entities with natural linkages across economics, public policy, research, and advocacy, and places that are adept at bringing issues like this into the spotlight in compelling ways. (A vivid recent example was the front-page *New York Times* treatment of Hoxby's and Christopher Avery's meticulously documented revelation of the failure of high-ability twelfth-graders even to apply to the nation's best colleges and universities.[6])

Among many questions that deserve deeper probing and tracking in the years ahead are these:

- Just how effective are the various forms of "gifted and talented" education at adding value to their students, both in the short run and over time? Programs range widely, from separate classes and schools to ability grouping within classrooms to "enrichment" activities of various kinds. Their impacts are likely as diverse as their approaches.

- Insofar as programs show positive effects, which elements matter? Curriculum? Instructors? Culture? Peer influence? Resources? Others?

- What are the advantages and disadvantages of various ways of identifying children for participation in gifted-education programs and how do these differ with children's ages or education levels?

- How successful is "differentiated instruction" at meeting the educational needs of high-ability students within conventional classrooms? What determines its success (e.g., teacher quality, teacher preparation, technology, relatively homogeneous classes)?

- What are the pros and cons—and effectiveness—of accelerating children's progress through K–12 education? How well does "mastery" (instead of traditional grade levels) work?

- What can be learned from other countries about the successful education of high-ability students?

Research and evaluation alone won't solve the neglect problem, but they can surely contribute to the development and implementation of workable solutions, provided that the political and policy will is there. This much is already clear: without that will and in the absence of focused attention, the United States is destined to continue under-educating vital parts of its human capital that could make enormous contributions to the country's future well-being.

Notes

1. Eric A. Hanushek, Paul E. Peterson, and Ludger Woessmann, "Achievement Growth: International and US State Trends in Student Performance," Harvard's Program on Education Policy and Governance and *Education Next*, July 2012, http:// www.hks.harvard.edu/pepg/PDF/Papers/PEPG12-03 _CatchingUp.pdf.

2. Caroline Hoxby and Christopher Avery, "The Missing 'One-Offs': The Hidden Supply of High-Achieving, Low-Income Students," Brookings Institution Press, Spring 2013, http:// www.brookings.edu/~/media/Projects/BPEA/Spring%202013 /2013a_hoxby.pdf.

3. This National Bureau of Economic Research working paper by Atila Abdulkadiroğlu, Joshua D. Angrist, and Parag A. Pathak ("The Elite Illusion: Achievement Effects at Boston and New York Exam Schools") describes very modest effects from selective-admission high schools in two US cities and also contains citations to most of the (very limited) research that has been done on this and related topics in the United States and internationally, http://www.nber.org/papers/w17264.

4. In the 18,647 high schools in the College Board database for 2012, for example, one third do not offer AP biology and barely half offer AP calculus, http://research.collegeboard.org /programs/ap/data/participation/2012.

5. Chester E. Finn Jr. and Jessica A. Hockett, *Exam Schools: Inside America's Most Selective Public High Schools* (Princeton, NJ: Princeton University Press, 2012), http://press .princeton.edu/titles/9811.html.

6. David Leonhardt, "Better Colleges Failing to Lure Talented Poor," *New York Times*, March 16, 2013, http://www.nytimes .com/2013/03/17/education/scholarly-poor-often-overlook -better-colleges.html?pagewanted=all&_r=1&.

Contributors

The Hoover Institution's Koret Task Force on K–12 Education currently includes the eleven members listed below:

John E. Chubb, a distinguished visiting fellow at the Hoover Institution, is the president of the National Association of Independent Schools. He served as the interim CEO of Education Sector, a nonprofit, nonpartisan research organization. He was previously a senior fellow at the Brookings Institution, a faculty member at Stanford University, and an adjunct professor at Johns Hopkins University and Princeton University. His books include *The Best Teachers in the World: Why We Don't Have Them and How We Could* (Hoover Institution Press, 2012), *Liberating Learning: Technology, Politics, and the Future of American Education* (Jossey-Bass, 2009), and *Politics, Markets, and America's Schools* (Brookings Institution Press, 1990), the last two with Terry M. Moe.

Williamson M. Evers, a research fellow at the Hoover Institution, was the US assistant secretary of education for policy from 2007 to 2009. In 2003, Evers served in Iraq as a senior adviser for education to Administrator L. Paul Bremer of the Coalition Provisional Authority. Evers has been a member of the National Educational Research Policy and Priorities Board, a commissioner on the California State Academic Standards Commission, a trustee on the Santa Clara County Board of Education, and president of the board of directors of the East Palo Alto Charter School.

Chester E. Finn Jr. is a senior fellow at the Hoover Institution and chairman of the task force. He is also president and trustee of the Thomas B. Fordham Foundation. Previously, he was professor of education and public policy at Vanderbilt University, senior fellow of the Hudson Institute, founding partner with the Edison Project, and legislative director for Senator Daniel P. Moynihan. He served as assistant US education secretary for research and improvement from 1985 to 1988. Author of more than four hundred articles and twenty books, Finn's most recent books are *Exam Schools: Inside America's Most Selective Public High Schools* (Princeton University Press, 2012) and *Reroute the Preschool Juggernaut* (Education Next Books, 2009).

Eric A. Hanushek is the Paul and Jean Hanna Senior Fellow in Education at the Hoover Institution. He is best known for introducing rigorous economic analysis into educational policy deliberations. He has produced twenty-one books and over two hundred scholarly articles. He is chairman of the Executive Committee for the Texas Schools Project at the University of Texas at Dallas and a research associate of the National Bureau of Economic Research. He formerly served as chair of the Board of Directors of the National Board for Education Sciences. His newest book, *Endangering Prosperity: A Global View of the American School* (Brookings Institution Press, 2013), documents the huge economic costs of continuing to have mediocre schools.

Paul T. Hill is a distinguished visiting fellow at the Hoover Institution. He is the founder and former director of the Center on Reinventing Public Education at the University of Washington. His most recent books are *Learning as We Go: Why School Choice is Worth the Wait* (Education Next Books, 2010) and *Charter Schools Against the Odds* (Education Next Books, 2006). He also contributed a chapter to *Private Vouchers* (Hoover Institution Press, 1995), a groundbreaking study edited by Terry M. Moe.

Caroline M. Hoxby is a senior fellow at the Hoover Institution, the Scott and Donya Bommer Professor of Economics at Stanford

University, the director of the Economics of Education Program at the National Bureau of Economic Research, and a presidential appointee to the National Board of Education Sciences. A public and labor economist, she is a leading scholar in the economics of education. Some of her research areas include the outcomes of graduates from different colleges, public school finance, school choice, and the effect of education on economic growth and income inequality. She is currently completing studies on how education affects economic growth, globalization in higher education, peer effects in education, and the effects of charter schools on student achievement.

Tom Loveless is a senior fellow at the Brown Center on Education Policy at the Brookings Institution. He researches education policy and reform and is author of *The Tracking Wars: State Reform Meets School Policy* (Brookings Institution Press, 1999) and editor of several books, most recently *Lessons Learned: What International Assessments Tell Us about Math Achievement* (Brookings Institution Press, 2007). Loveless's teaching experience includes nine years as a sixth-grade teacher in California and seven years as assistant and associate professor of public policy at the John F. Kennedy School of Government, Harvard University.

Terry M. Moe is a senior fellow at the Hoover Institution and the William Bennett Munro Professor of Political Science at Stanford University. He has written extensively on the politics and reform of American education. His newest book, *Special Interest: Teachers Unions and America's Public Schools* (Brookings Institution Press, 2011), provides the first comprehensive study of the teachers' unions and their impacts on the nation's schools. His past work on education includes *Politics, Markets, and America's Schools* (Brookings Institution Press, 1990) and *Liberating Learning: Technology, Politics, and the Future of American Education* (Jossey-Bass, 2009), both with John Chubb, and *Schools, Vouchers, and the American Public* (Brookings Institution Press, 2001). As a political scientist, Moe's research interests extend well beyond public education. He has written extensively on political institutions, public bureaucracy, and the presidency and has been an influential contributor to those fields.

Paul E. Peterson is a senior fellow at the Hoover Institution and editor in chief of *Education Next: A Journal of Opinion and Research.* He is also the Henry Lee Shattuck Professor of Government and director of the Program on Education Policy and Governance at Harvard University. He is the author of *Saving Schools: From Horace Mann to Digital Learning* (Belknap/Harvard, 2010) and a co-author of *Endangering Prosperity: A Global View of the American School* (Brookings Institution Press, 2013) and *Teachers Versus the Public: What Americans Think about Their Schools and School Reform* (forthcoming, 2014).

Herbert J. Walberg, a distinguished visiting fellow at the Hoover Institution, taught for thirty-five years at Harvard and at the University of Illinois at Chicago. Author or editor of more than seventy books, he has written extensively for educational and psychological scholarly journals on measuring and raising student achievement and human accomplishments. His most recent book is *Tests, Testing, and Genuine School Reform* (Education Next Books, 2011). He was appointed a member of the National Assessment Governing Board and the National Board for Educational Sciences and is a fellow of several scholarly groups, including the American Association for the Advancement of Science, the International Academy of Education, and the Royal Statistical Society. He chairs the Beck Foundation and the Heartland Institute.

Grover "Russ" Whitehurst is the Brown Chair, senior fellow, and director of the Brown Center on Education Policy at the Brookings Institution, where he is responsible for shaping public and political opinion on education policy based on findings from research. As the first director of the Institute of Education Sciences within the US Department of Education, he is widely acknowledged to have had a transforming effect on the quality of education research. In his earlier career as a professor of developmental psychology, he carried out seminal research on early literacy, language development, and preschool education. A program he developed to enhance language development in children from low-income families, Dialogic Reading, is used in preschools around the world. He is a pioneer in delivering college-level instruction through the Internet, in recognition of which he received the Microsoft Innovators in Higher Education Award.

This volume was co-edited by:

Richard Sousa, senior associate director and research fellow at the Hoover Institution, is an economist who specializes in human capital, discrimination, labor market issues, and K–12 education. He co-authored *School Figures: The Data behind the Debate* (Hoover Institution Press, 2003) and co-edited *Reacting to the Spending Spree: Policy Changes We Can Afford* (Hoover Institution Press, 2009), an assessment of the government's response to the economic crisis of 2008–09. Sousa was responsible for launching the Institution's major communications initiatives, including the *Hoover Digest, Education Next, Policy Review,* and *Uncommon Knowledge.* From 1990 to 1995, he directed the Institution's Diplomat Training Program. He served as director of the Hoover Institution Library and Archives from 2007 to 2012 and was responsible for major acquisitions, including the Chiang Kai-shek diaries; the William Rehnquist papers; the Georgian, Estonian, and Lithuanian KGB files; and the Ba'th Party collection.

About the Hoover Institution's
KORET TASK FORCE ON K–12 EDUCATION

The Hoover Institution's Koret Task Force on K–12 Education is made up of experts in the field of education. Brought together by the Hoover Institution, Stanford University, with the support of the Koret Foundation and other foundations and individuals, the task force examines the prospects and options for education reform in the United States. Its primary objectives are to gather, evaluate, and disseminate existing evidence in an analytic context and to analyze reform measures that will enhance the quality and productivity of K–12 education.

The task force includes some of the most highly regarded and best-known education scholars in the nation, many of whom have served in executive and advisory roles for federal, state, and local governments and as professors at the country's leading universities. Their combined expertise represents more than three hundred years of research and study in the field of education.

The task force is the centerpiece of the Hoover Institution's Initiative on American Educational Institutions and Academic Performance. In addition to producing original research, analysis, and recommendations in a growing body of work on the most important issues in American education today, task force members serve as editors, contributors, and members of the editorial board of *Education Next: A Journal of Opinion and Research*, published by the Hoover Institution. For further information, see the task force website at **www.hoover.org/taskforces/education**.

BOOKS OF RELATED INTEREST
FROM THE KORET TASK FORCE ON K–12 EDUCATION

Endangering Prosperity: A Global View of the American School, by Eric A. Hanushek, Paul E. Peterson, and Ludger Woessmann (Brookings Institution Press, 2013)

The Best Teachers in the World: Why We Don't Have Them and How We Could, by John E. Chubb (Hoover Institution Press, 2012)

Exam Schools: Inside America's Most Selective Public High Schools, by Chester E. Finn Jr. and Jessica A. Hockett (Princeton University Press, 2012)

Choice and Federalism: Defining the Federal Role in Education, by the Koret Task Force (Hoover Institution Press, 2012)

Tests, Testing, and Genuine School Reform, by Herbert J. Walberg (Education Next Books, 2011)

American Education in 2030, by the Koret Task Force (2010), PDF e-book, http://www.hoover.org/taskforces/education/AE2030

Saving Schools: From Horace Mann to Virtual Learning, by Paul E. Peterson (The Belknap Press of Harvard University Press, 2010)

Learning as We Go: Why School Choice is Worth the Wait, by Paul T. Hill (Education Next Books, 2010)

Advancing Student Achievement, by Herbert J. Walberg (Education Next Books, 2010)

Reroute the Preschool Juggernaut, by Chester E. Finn Jr. (Education Next Books, 2009)

Liberating Learning: Technology, Politics, and the Future of American Education, by Terry M. Moe and John E. Chubb (Jossey-Bass, 2009)

Learning from No Child Left Behind: How and Why the Nation's Most Important but Controversial Education Law Should Be Renewed, by John E. Chubb (Education Next Books, 2009)

Courting Failure: How School Finance Lawsuits Exploit Judges' Good Intentions and Harm Our Children, edited by Eric A. Hanushek (Education Next Books, 2006)

Charter Schools against the Odds: An Assessment by the Koret Task Force on K–12 Education, edited by Paul T. Hill (Education Next Books, 2006)

Reforming Education in Florida: A Study Prepared by the Koret Task Force on K–12 Education, edited by Paul E. Peterson (Hoover Institution Press, 2006)

Reforming Education in Arkansas: Recommendations from the Koret Task Force, by the Koret Task Force (Hoover Institution Press, 2005)

Within Our Reach: How America Can Educate Every Child, edited by John E. Chubb (Rowman & Littlefield Publishers, 2005)

Reforming Education in Texas: Recommendations from the Koret Task Force, by the Koret Task Force (Hoover Institution Press, 2004)

Our Schools and Our Future . . . Are We Still at Risk?, edited by Paul E. Peterson (Hoover Institution Press, 2003)

Choice with Equity, edited by Paul T. Hill (Hoover Institution Press, 2002)

School Accountability: An Assessment by the Koret Task Force on K–12 Education, edited by Williamson M. Evers and Herbert J. Walberg (Hoover Institution Press, 2002)

A Primer on America's Schools, edited by Terry M. Moe (Hoover Institution Press, 2001)

Index